So Fill Our Imaginations

So Fill Our Imaginations

The Work and Play of a Year of Preaching

Mark Lloyd Taylor

WIPF & STOCK · Eugene, Oregon

SO FILL OUR IMAGINATIONS
The Work and Play of a Year of Preaching

Copyright © 2022 Mark Lloyd Taylor. All rights reserved. Except for brief quotations in critical publications or reviews, no part of this book may be reproduced in any manner without prior written permission from the publisher. Write: Permissions, Wipf and Stock Publishers, 199 W. 8th Ave., Suite 3, Eugene, OR 97401.

Wipf & Stock
An Imprint of Wipf and Stock Publishers
199 W. 8th Ave., Suite 3
Eugene, OR 97401

www.wipfandstock.com

PAPERBACK ISBN: 978-1-6667-3595-6
HARDCOVER ISBN: 978-1-6667-9366-6
EBOOK ISBN: 978-1-6667-9367-3

03/10/22

Cover art: Susan Feiker, "The Great Faith of the Canaanite Woman."

All Scripture quotations are from the New Revised Standard Version, copyright © 1989 by the Division of Christian Education of the National Council of Churches of Christ in the USA. Used by permission. All rights reserved.

Photo of St. Paul's upstairs worship space, copyright © Lara Swimmer; reproduced with permission.

Photo of St. Paul's baptismal font, copyright © Lara Swimmer; reproduced with permission.

Image of *kintsugi* (#1805501275) purchased from Shutterstock (www.shutterstock.com) and reproduced under license #SSTK-0D9EB-F937.

Image of Yeesook Yung's adaptation of *kintsugi* (#645410143) purchased from Shutterstock (www.shutterstock.com) and reproduced under license #SSTK-0D9EB-F937.

Images of Christian church with cross (#86245006) and courthouse with American flag (#332719761) purchased from Adobe Stock (https://stock.adobe.com) and reproduced under license AE00545313575CUS.

Image of golden arches of McDonald's (#1324330487) purchased from Shutterstock (www.shutterstock.com) and reproduced under license #SSTK-0D9EB-F937.

Contents

List of Illustrations | vii
Preface | ix
Acknowledgments | xi

Introduction: Contexts and Texts for a Year of Preaching | 1

1. Seeing the Signs—The Fourth Sunday of Advent | 21
2. Walking Makes the Way—The Third Sunday after the Epiphany | 33
3. Beyond the Fences—The Conversion of St. Paul the Apostle | 44
4. Coming by Night, Being Born to Daylight [Remarks for Shared Homily]—The Second Sunday in Lent | 53
5. Touching Is Believing [Remarks for Shared Homily]—The Second Sunday of Easter | 62
6. To an Unknown God in Whom We Live and Move and Have Our Being—The Sixth Sunday of Easter | 66
7. Compassion: Visceral, Face-to-Face and Hands-On, Limitlessly Expansive [Remarks for Shared Homily]—The Second Sunday after Pentecost | 77
8. Let Both of Them Grow Together until the Harvest [Remarks for Shared Homily]—The Seventh Sunday after Pentecost | 83

9. The Conversion of Jesus—The Eleventh Sunday after Pentecost | 93

10. Refusing to Play the Payback Game [Remarks for Shared Homily]—The Fifteenth Sunday after Pentecost | 105

11. Stewarding Our Worth and Inclusion, with Anne Hill Thomson—The Nineteenth Sunday after Pentecost | 110

12. Mending What Fear Has Buried [Remarks for Shared Homily]—The Twenty-Fourth Sunday after Pentecost | 119

Conclusion: The Work and Play of Preaching | 128

Epilogue: Preaching to (My) White Privilege | 145

Bibliography | 151

List of Illustrations

Figure 1. St. Paul's Upstairs Worship Space—photo © Lara Swimmer | 7

Figure 2. Sunday Evenings at St. Paul's (Downstairs)—photo by Jesse Smith, from the collection of St. Paul's Episcopal Church | 9

Figure 3. Social/Political/Economic Context—word cloud by author | 16

Figure 4. St. Paul's Baptismal Font—photo © Lara Swimmer | 68

Figure 5. *The Great Faith of the Canaanite Woman*—painting by Susan Feiker, from author's collection—photo by author | 101

Figure 6. *Kintsugi*—photo purchased from Shutterstock | 123

Figure 7. Yeesook Yung's Adaptation of *Kintsugi*—photo purchased from Shutterstock | 125

Figures 8 and 9. Wondering and Wandering with Matthew 15—from author's sketchbook | 131–32

Figure 10. Between the Cross and the Stars and Stripes—collage by author of photos purchased from Adobe Stock and Shutterstock | 136

Figure 11. *Mary of Bethany—Letting Down and Lavishing in Love*—drawing by author | 148

Preface

Almighty and eternal God,
so draw our hearts to you,
so guide our minds,
so fill our imaginations,
so control our wills,
that we may be wholly yours,
utterly dedicated to you;
and then use us, we pray, as you will,
and always to your glory and the welfare of your people.[1]

THAT'S THE PRAYER OF preparation—or self-dedication—altar servers and preachers, lay and ordained, recite together before the Sunday morning masses at St. Paul's Episcopal Church (Seattle, Washington) during Advent and Lent, along with a responsive reading of Psalm 84:1–9. Throughout the rest of the church year, we prepare ourselves for Holy Eucharist using a different psalm and two other short prayers. I particularly like the version above and wish we prayed it more often. It's the line "so fill our

---

1. Episcopal Church, *Book of Common Prayer*, 832–33. This prayer comes from Archbishop William Temple; see Hatchett, *Commentary*, 568.

Preface

imaginations" that entices me most. "So control our wills," on the other hand, proves troublesome—although I've tried to sit with it attentively. I even wrote the following little entry in my journal: "so *control* our wills—maybe not in a punitive or pre-emptive/constraining way, but as in: hold strong to the rudder because of the current or the winds." In any case, I still find "so fill our imaginations" more attractive and delightful.

For better or for worse, there's an indirectness to my preaching. I can't imagine setting out to control my hearers' wills, if that were even possible for one human being in relation to another. I'm not sure about guiding their minds, either. Maybe drawing their hearts in some collaborative, non-ultimate sense. But preaching as in part about filling a corner or an empty space of the gathered assembly's imaginations—that resonates. Because, for better or worse, such a spiritual and homiletical stance coheres with the feminist and womanist and process theologies that have formed me. More to the point, my own personal access to anything remotely approximating self-dedication to God comes through my imagination. Not my will. Not primarily through my mind or even my heart. There's a liberating indirectness to images. They are given to us. They are ours. We don't need to take them. They are already ours, even if we don't know what they are. But we can play with them and allow them to go to work filling corners and empty spaces. Then, as a result, we may find ourselves feeling and thinking and doing and being differently.

Preaching. Images and imagination. The parables of Jesus. A Godly Play lesson. Poems. A broken porcelain bowl mended with gold. A seven-foot-tall assemblage of no-longer-buried-in-the-ground kimchi pots. A story. A blogpost. A movie or two. The vocabulary and structure of a Gospel text. People walking. Walking a long way: Jesus with Peter, Andrew, James, and John as companions; or short: Donald Trump all by himself. An icon of the great faith of the Canaanite woman, great enough to convert Jesus. Every single one of us a little baby Sophia, living and moving and having our being in the universal womb of God, our mother.

Wednesday in the Third Week of Advent
December 15, 2021

Acknowledgments

WITHOUT MY PEOPLE, THERE would be no book. Two groups of people: the people of St. Paul's Episcopal Church in Seattle and my students, colleagues, and friends at Seattle University.

Thank you, people of St. Paul's, for surrounding and supporting me all these years as we have worshipped together, spoken and moved about and kept silence and stillness, planned and been surprised, laughed and cried, centered in and reached out. Thank you for listening to me preach across a church year, a year of life in the world. Better: thank you for coaxing these sermons out of me and then giving them space to live on for a while. Special thanks to those of you who gave me permission to share your playful work and working play with the readers of this book. To Anne Hill Thomson and Daniel Tidwell-Davis for your sermons. To Anne Doe-Overstreet for your poem. To Melissa (Missy) Trull for collaborating with me on the Godly Play lesson. To Susan Feiker for writing the icon. To baby Sophia's parents for her story and yours. People of St. Paul's, as we carefully reopen for in-person worship after sixteen months of COVID-19-imposed absence, I've missed you more than I can say.

Friends at school—colleagues and students—thank you for coming to church with me in and around my year of preaching. Thanks especially to you students who have stretched me most, because your life experience brings such difference to mine. Traditional Roman Catholics; you women who pray the Chaplet of Divine Mercy. Veterans of the wars in Iraq and

Acknowledgments

Afghanistan. Friends of color. Unitarian Universalists who take such courses as "Jesus *the* Christ" (!) and "God, Creation, and *Trinity*" (!!) with me. All of you shape my teaching and my preaching in irreplaceable ways. I'm grateful to staff member Rhea Panela for making a more pleasing and effective image out of my rough, hand-lettered word cloud.

And then there are the four dear people who were generous enough with their time and talent to read a first draft of this book: Rev. Sara Fischer, Rev. Alissabeth Newton, Rt. Rev. Dr. Edward Donalson III, and Dr. Debra-L. Sequeira. Sara, thanks to you for your leadership as rector of St. Paul's during the composition and delivery, reception and initial agency of these twelve sermons, for allowing me to excerpt from your own preaching, and for your skills as copy editor and memoir-writing coach. To you, Alissa, for gently and lovingly trying to check my tendencies toward St. Paul's exceptionalism; if there's still too much here, you are not at fault. Edward, if this book manages to reach non-Episcopalians, I owe you much of the credit; thanks for your questions and suggestions. Edward and Alissa both, thank you for inviting me to be more forthcoming about my social location and my vocation as lay preacher.

Finally, and *first* of all, Debra. Thanks so much for our twenty-four years of marriage, and counting. We *are* a team! Thanks for finding St. Paul's with me when we set out together to look for a church home. In my humble but accurate opinion, you are the most gracious, most beautiful eucharistic minister ever to don the tunicle at St. Paul's and sing the prayers of the people and proffer us the blood of Christ, the cup of salvation. Your inclusive leadership as professor, department chair, associate dean, and dean at Seattle Pacific University has inspired my own academic career. Your scholarship in sociolinguistics and the ethnography of communication provides a most stimulating conversation partner for my work. Among so many, many other things, thanks for being the very first reader of this book—and for always reminding me that I care more about my pet projects than others do (like my questing after Melville and his novel about that whale). But seriously, what a comfort to know you were watching over me from upstairs—even as you slept—all those early mornings when I was downstairs writing at this our kitchen table. I love you!

Introduction

Contexts and Texts for a Year of Preaching

I AM AN OCCASIONAL preacher. For my day job, I teach at Seattle University's School of Theology and Ministry—an academic enterprise that offers a portfolio of graduate degrees, from the traditional master of divinity to less ecclesially-oriented programs in couples and family therapy and transformational leadership, with a doctor of ministry recently tossed into the mix. I am *not* a deacon, priest, or bishop in the Episcopal Church, which means my preaching arises out of my baptismal identity rather than ordination. But I hold a PhD in systematic theology and—to get a little granular with the polity of the Episcopal Church—I am a licensed lay preacher in the Diocese of Olympia. And so, I *do* preach occasionally, most often within the context of St. Paul's Episcopal Church in Seattle, Washington. I have been a member of the parish for twenty-three years.

Although I have been preaching at St. Paul's since 2000, that work, that play, took on a more regular rhythm and shape during the church year that stretched from November 27, 2016, to December 2, 2017. Basically, it fell out that I was scheduled to preach once a month on Sundays throughout the year—six times at the 5:00 p.m. mass; the other six at 7:30, 9:00, and 11:15 a.m. (the same homilist almost always preached the same sermon at all three morning services), most often on the third Sunday of each month. Looking back at these twelve sermons later sparked the idea of gathering them up, wrapping them in a memoir around their composition and delivery, reception and subsequent agency—which doubles as an exercise in theological reflection upon preaching itself—and offering the results to you, my readers.

It never would have occurred to me to do so with any other twelve (or seven or forty-four) of my sermons chosen according to some thematic of my own devising. I make no claim that they are representative of my preaching voice. That they are good sermons—or my best, heaven forbid. I'm not trying to craft a legacy of preaching. No. These twelve sermons belong together because they make their way slowly and steadily through the calendar of a single church year, because they weave themselves into and out of the fixed pattern of Scripture readings appointed ahead of time by the Sunday lectionary followed in the Episcopal Church. What's more, the memoir/theological reflection aspect of this book has as much to do with St. Paul's—its physical plant, people, liturgical customs, and homiletical expectations—as it does with my own life. And wider still, the multilayered realities of neighborhood, city, country, and world show up throughout. You have before you a personal theological and spiritual memoir, to be sure. But it's also a social/political/economic one. Communal. Global and national and local. Reflections upon the work and play of preaching across a turbulent and supersaturated year of life in the world.

St. Paul's

The St. Paul's Episcopal Church (Seattle) website proclaims: "St. Paul's is an accepting, progressive Anglo-Catholic parish renewing people for their Christian lives in the world through worship, spiritual formation, engagement with the arts, life in community, and acts of compassion."[1] Other recent self-descriptions have included: "[St. Paul's is] a place of prayer where the senses are fully engaged in the worship of God; . . . where ancient ritual speaks to the experience of today's life"; and "We are urban and diverse—a little funky (adults and children, young and old, women and men, gay and straight, single, partnered, and married); exploring how to enact justice and compassion locally and globally."[2]

Textbook discussions of Anglo-Catholicism refer back to the Oxford or Tractarian Movement in England with its emphasis on "the continuity of Anglicanism with ancient Christianity, [the attempt] to reconnect

---

1. Home page of St. Paul's Episcopal Church, http://www.stpaulseattle.org, accessed Nov. 6, 2019.
2. St. Paul's Episcopal Church, *Renewing St. Paul's*, 2.

Introduction

Anglicanism with its medieval Catholic roots . . . [and] the importance of liturgy and traditional Christian doctrine."[3] Again, according to St. Paul's own website:

> St. Paul's is an Anglo-Catholic parish, a more specific expression of the Anglican/Episcopal Church that arose out of particular historical circumstances. Rooted in the retention of Catholic Christianity within the English reformation, Anglo-Catholicism emerged as a dissident movement within an eighteenth-century church that had so absorbed the rationalism of its time that it had lost sight of the importance of the sacraments and of the centrality of an experience of awe and wonder in the spiritual life. As Anglo-Catholics, our ultimate worship experience is one in which we not only glimpse but enter into and taste something of the beauty and mystery of God. About 10 percent of parishes in the Episcopal Church call themselves Anglo-Catholic. The following are elements that exist in many of these parishes: Sacramental . . . ; Prayerful . . . ; Surrounded by a Great Cloud of Witnesses . . . ; Reverential, Expressed through Music, the Senses and the Body . . . ; Committed to Beauty and Justice Together.[4]

That last phrase, "beauty and justice together," hints at something often underemphasized both in books and popular perception. Early Anglo-Catholic leaders in England and America rejected any nostalgic, romanticist infatuation with things medieval and instead—amidst the misery and poverty of the industrial cities and towns and neighborhoods of their nineteenth century—called for the recovery of the communal dimension and social mission of the church of the first five centuries that stood over against Roman imperial power.[5] That's why they championed the beauty of weekly, sacramental worship. That's why they built churches in factory districts and slums: precisely to remind the laboring poor that they were surrounded and embraced by God where they lived and worked. For the fundamental theo-logic of pioneering Anglo-Catholics insisted that God's incarnation in/as Jesus effects both the humanization of the divine and the deification of the human, especially those dehumanized by the dominant social/political/economic power of the emerging new nineteenth-century empire: industrial capitalism.

3. Campbell, *Christian Confessions*, 129–30. See also Holmes, *Brief History*, 103–12.
4. St. Paul's Episcopal Church, "Anglo-Catholicism."
5. Franklin's excellent article, "Pusey and Worship," helps tell this part of the story of Anglo-Catholicism.

Hence, the modifiers "accepting" and "progressive" with respect to Anglo-Catholic are *crucial* to St. Paul's identity, even if they always remain *aspirational*. For decades, the parish has attempted to provide a safe place for LGBTQ+ folk to worship, to be in Christian community—often to return to church and heal from the wounds inflicted by other Christian congregations and denominations. In the 1980s, St. Paul's was one of the first religious communities in the region to minister actively and publicly to men with AIDS, living and deceased. An openly gay and partnered man, the Rev. Morrie Hauge, was called and served as rector (= pastor) in the 1990s and early 2000s. What joy when the State of Washington legalized same-sex marriages, and the Episcopal Church authorized liturgies blessing such unions! Furthermore, unlike some Anglo-Catholic parishes and other institutions with their opposition to women's ordination, St. Paul's has sought out female leadership and flourished by way of it. The past two rectors of the parish have been women: The Rev. Melissa Skelton (later, after serving as bishop and archbishop in the Anglican Church of Canada, The Most Rev. Skelton) and The Rev. Sara Fischer. Lore has it that the first female vestry member in the diocese was elected by St. Paul's (vestry = congregational board). A female deacon also ministered at the parish early on after the Episcopal Church opened that ministry to women. In both cases, this pioneering woman was one and the same Mary Drew.

St. Paul's began as a log-cabin mission in 1892, then constructed a church building at its current location in the Lower Queen Anne neighborhood of Seattle in 1903. A structure housing chapel, church offices, and education rooms was added in the 1930s. By the late 1950s, the parish had purchased property on top of Queen Anne Hill, a more suburban-like, residential area, with the goal of relocating there from its already busy, gritty location. A new rector, however, led the congregation to reverse those plans and remain at 15 Roy Street, staying connected to urban Seattle, recommitted to being a reconciling presence in a place with many challenges, needs, and opportunities. The charge of its patron, St. Paul, to "go into the city and you will be told what you must do" (Acts 9:6), served as an emblem of this decision and adorned parish letterhead for years. A new building for worship was built and consecrated in 1963—in a dramatic Pacific Northwest-inflected mid-century modern style—during the Seattle World's Fair just a few blocks away. The fairgrounds have since become the Seattle Center, a major tourist and artistic destination, today encompassing the opera house, professional theaters, museums, the city's indoor sports and concert venue, and the iconic Space Needle.

Introduction

I was there at 5:00 p.m. on Sunday, September 27, 2009, the Feast of St. Michael and All Angels (transferred), when St. Paul's launched a new weekly celebration of the Holy Eucharist. Growth in attendance at the principal morning mass created a felt need for this third Sunday liturgy. Equally important, it provided an opportunity to gather new people to the parish, especially young people in their twenties and thirties and those unable or disinclined to worship at an Episcopal Church on Sunday morning. The goal was to create a eucharistic service that neither copied the Sunday morning liturgies nor departed jarringly from the parish's established pattern of liturgical life. The result, Sunday Evenings at St. Paul's, meets in the more intimate worship space of a refurbished parish hall, with altar at the center of the room, assembly and liturgical ministers seated around. The service features inclusive and expansive language, a distinctive jazz-driven musical style and repertoire, a "shared homily," engagement with artists-in-residence, and significant time of fellowship that opens out to the work of justice and compassion. The practice of a *shared* homily is particularly germane to my preaching, as I shall indicate in a moment.[6]

But we need to back up a little. St. Paul's called Melissa Skelton as rector in 2005 and asked her to lead the congregation in securing membership growth (especially among families with children) and greater financial stability, while at the same time strengthening the parish's rich tradition of Anglo-Catholic worship and Benedictine rhythms of prayer. In addition to the 5:00 p.m. Sunday Eucharist, this effort eventuated in a renovation of the 1963 worship space. Three pairs of values expressed the aims of the renovation: visibility and accessibility, identity and hospitality, beauty and flexibility. Notable changes included an expanded glass entryway surrounding a new baptismal font with flowing water and accommodating full immersion of adults and children, visibly signaling to the cars and pedestrians on Roy Street the centrality of baptism to Christian life in the world; a freestanding altar designed by the same artist who created the font; new windows in the nave in Northwest blues, greens, and golds; improved lighting; refinished pews, benches, and credence table; new chancel flooring; and more harmonious paint on the altar wall. The renovated worship space was first used on Christmas Eve 2011.[7] Although this was two years after the launch of Sunday Evenings at St. Paul's, the two projects were intimately connected.

---

6. Should you wish more information about St. Paul's Sunday evening mass, please consult the article I cowrote with Alissabeth Newton, "Praying at the Edges."

7. The architect for the renovation has published an article on the project: Jones,

For by 2008, meanwhile, after three years of leadership from Mother Skelton, average Sunday attendance at St. Paul's had doubled. The 10:30 a.m. mass was beginning to feel uncomfortably full to some. The parish had also become more intentional about its Anglo-Catholic identity and more confident in seeking to make its spiritual and liturgical gifts accessible to a wider group of people. And so both as response to and catalyst for growth and as a means to advance its mission, the parish embarked on a congregational development process that culminated in the third Sunday liturgy. Town hall meetings were held to discuss the experience of numerical growth. A small group of clergy and laypeople formed a planning team—led by the rector, commissioned by the vestry, and supported by a diocesan grant. Their work fell into four areas: worship space and furnishings, liturgy and music, community development, and communications. As mentioned above, the Sunday evening mass was held for the first time in September 2009. Over the next couple of years, Sunday attendance continued to grow—requiring additional liturgical expansion. So, along with the 5:00 p.m. liturgy, St. Paul's moved to offer three Sunday morning masses (at 7:30, 9:00, and 11:15). And for several years, St. Paul's also hosted the weekly bilingual Spanish-English Eucharist of Our Lady of Guadalupe Episcopal Church at 1:30 p.m. on Sundays.

Preaching at St. Paul's

If you ask what it's like to preach at St. Paul's these days, what norms and expectations both cajole and constrain the preacher, I would have to say: it depends. Depends upon whether we are talking about preaching upstairs at the Sunday morning masses or downstairs on Sunday evenings. The two worship spaces differ dramatically in size, design, layout, and furnishings.

Upstairs, the renovated 1963 church traces an exaggerated A-frame at a pitch of eighty degrees with large wooden piers on the side aisles marking out triangular bays. Amazing verticality comes coupled with the more compact footprint of the nave. The interior peak of the roofline—with its five skylights—towers sixty feet above the floor, while the congregation occupies a space just some forty feet square. Transcendence *and* immanence? Despite the spareness and angularity of its mid-century modern design, the worship space used on Sunday mornings is fairly traditional in terms of center aisle and two side aisles, with slip pews fixed to the floor in between. Maximum seating capacity is about two hundred. A chancel up front on a

---

"Forest in the City."

Introduction

raised platform contains pulpit, altar, benches for vested liturgical ministers (anywhere from two to nine, depending on which mass), and a credence table. Unusually, and jarringly when visitors first catch wind of it, the organ and choir loft hang suspended from the ceiling in back above the entryway—with no load-bearing support from below. Compared to many Episcopal, let alone Roman Catholic, to say nothing of Eastern Orthodox churches, the upstairs worship space is remarkably devoid of pictorial and figurative features. True, you can't miss the huge wooden crucifix—with the larger-than-life corpus of Jesus Christ—high up on the altar wall. And the pulpit provides an exception that proves the rule, as we shall see. But otherwise, the windows in the bays on the side aisles consist solely of translucent glass shingles in muted colors. No figures. No words. Only two icons hang in the nave: one of mother Mary and baby Jesus (the Virgin of the Sign from Isaiah 7:14), the other of St. Paul the Apostle, patron of the house. An icon of St. Michael the Archangel watches over the comings and goings in the entryway. That's it! Even the terra-cotta stations of the cross and the bronze tabernacle that matches font and altar are marked with very simple visual elements (a pair of dice, human eyes with tears, an unadorned cross).

St. Paul's Upstairs Worship Space

So Fill Our Imaginations

By contrast, the 5:00 p.m. Sunday liturgy gathers *downstairs* in the parish hall, directly beneath the nave where the morning masses are held. The ceiling is low and anchors ductwork for heating and ventilation. A storage area sits to the north of the worship space, hidden by a folding, accordion-like screen. The parish kitchen lies behind wooden panels and a sliding door at the south end of the room. Worshippers access the space by way of a dedicated gate and outside ramp a few dozen feet west of the main doors to the (upstairs) church. As phase 1 of the building renovation, the ramp was rebuilt to be smoother, gentler, and safer, while the parish hall itself was repaired, repainted, and refurbished. Floor-to-ceiling clear glass windows look east on to the Bolster Memorial Garden where the ashes of departed parishioners are interred. The terraced garden is green all year round with small trees, ornamental shrubs and grasses, perennials, and annuals. A smaller green space borders the entrance ramp and is visible through windows atop the west wall.

A purpose-built wooden altar thirty-eight inches tall and thirty-six inches square stands in the center of the room. At one end of a diagonal axis bisecting the room, a presider's chair is placed; at the other end, a wooden lectern—both facing the altar. Worshippers and assisting ministers sit in a circle (or rounded diamond with four quadrants) around the altar facing in toward one another on stackable wood and metal chairs. Once, on a Christmas Eve, over seventy-five people were accommodated for worship in this downstairs (5:00 p.m.) set. Nowadays, on most Sunday evenings, chairs are provided for forty to fifty worshippers. A grand piano sits in the northwest corner, a Mary shrine opposite up against the windows to the Bolster Garden. The shrine consists of a large printed and framed image of the Virgin of Vladimir behind a low wooden table supporting a bowl of sand into which candles can be placed by worshippers. All these furnishings, *all of them*, must be set up from scratch and removed completely and placed in storage by the community each Sunday evening to accommodate the many other uses of the space throughout the week.

Upstairs, on Sunday morning, the preacher stands somewhat distant from the assembly. Alone. Only the preacher *stands* during the sermon. A step up from the floor of the nave into the chancel, demarcated by a communion rail. Then up in the pulpit a further three steps. Innovative in design and appearance, with its five blue-and-black enameled metal panels set in a wooden framework, the upstairs pulpit is nevertheless functionally traditional. Inside, it provides an angled desktop-like surface and lower

Introduction

shelf for papers (sermon manuscript and worship bulletin), books, a glass of water, small visual aids the preacher might hold aloft, and so on. From the front, from the assembly's vantage point, that is, the pulpit resembles the prow of a ship.

Sunday Evenings at St. Paul's (Downstairs)

There is no pulpit—prow-like or otherwise—for the downstairs preacher. At 5:00 p.m. on Sundays, the preacher preaches *seated* along with everyone else in the room. The preacher, the presider, the vested assisting ministers are not physically separated from the assembly but part of the same circle—rubbing shoulders with the people sitting next to them. *All* find themselves equally around the altar and across from one another. If the 5:00 p.m. preacher is also the priest-presider, they facilitate the shared homily from the presider's chair (which differs from the other wood and metal chairs only in having arms). When someone else preaches, layperson or clergy, they move their chair in front of the lectern just after the Gospel reading and preach seated from that place. Whatever notes or outline or manuscript or electronic device or book or pictures or other items the preacher plans on using during the shared homily must be held in their hands or balanced on their lap or placed and fetched and replaced on the floor in front of or beside them. The lectern in the downstairs worship space, with its angled desktop and shelf, is reserved for use by layfolk for the two readings from Scripture and for the proclamation of the Gospel by deacon or priest.

Current expectations at St. Paul's call for sermons during the morning masses to be twelve minutes in length, maybe a bit more. There is *no* expectation, however, as in some Episcopal parishes, that all three Scripture readings be mentioned in a given sermon. It's enough to have them read aloud and in the air. Literally in the air, because we do not provide printed copies of the readings along with or as part of the Sunday morning worship bulletin. And neither the red book, nor the blue one, in the pews is a Bible (instead, the 1979 Book of Common Prayer and *Hymnal 1982*, respectively). In an Anglo-Catholic environment like St. Paul's, with its emphasis on the full engagement of all the human senses in worshipping God, Scripture shows up as an *aural* event. This is why I list out all the Scripture readings for each Sunday morning occasion below (including the psalm), even if they don't all figure in the sermon. I do so to acknowledge their embodied presence in the space and time surrounding my preaching. Moreover, at St. Paul's, there is a strong privileging of the Gospel reading upstairs on Sunday mornings, visually, spatially, liturgically, by way of a procession with torches and incense down from the chancel and altar into the midst of the assembly (midway up the center aisle) where the Gospel is proclaimed.

During my year of occasional preaching considered here, the regular preachers on Sunday mornings at St. Paul's were Mother Sara Fischer (the rector of the parish and a priest, of course) and Deacon Stephen Crippen. Father Rob Rhodes, as new associate rector, joined the preaching lineup toward the end of the church year. Two of the parish's priest associates, Fathers Jay Rozendaal and Walt Knowles, preached less frequently than I did. Whoever the preacher, there *is* a strong expectation that Sunday morning sermons at St. Paul's will be delivered *orally* with grace and skill and conviction from that ship-prow pulpit mentioned earlier (whether from full manuscript or, more rarely, from a "sermon map" or outline) and then be posted as a polished *literary text* on the parish website sometime the following week.[8]

Perhaps the most significant and intentional innovation downstairs at 5:00 p.m. on Sundays, beyond the physical space itself, is the "shared

---

8. See http://www.stpaulseattle.org/sermons/. I go one step further in this book by converting the informal list of resources crediting the work of others at the end of my sermons posted online to proper footnote citations.

Introduction

homily." The preacher, whether priest, deacon, or one of a group of laypersons, offers seven minutes or so of orienting remarks, drawing a single, clear theme or issue out of one or more of the Scripture readings. Then instead of wrapping everything up beautifully and symmetrically, they pose a few wondering questions about what it might mean, to which anyone in the room can respond with a brief comment. *Brief* responses, not long disquisitions. *Responses* to the preacher's words, *reflections* on any of the Scripture readings for the evening, or on the occasion in the church year, the life of the person, the parish, the nation, the world. The shared homily is *not* meant to be free group therapy. Each response is allowed to stand on its own—no crosstalk, no dialogue. The presider calls the shared homily to an end with the ringing of a bell, followed by silence and stillness, before all rise to sing the Nicene Creed. The group of additional voices preaching on Sunday evenings—better, opening up the *community's* shared homily—is larger than that upstairs in the morning. A half a dozen or more. Predominantly female voices, along with a pair of self-identified queer ones.

For the longest time, preachers at the 5:00 p.m. mass resisted having their remarks reduced to writing and posted to the parish website, believing that the shared homily renders preaching in the evening improvisational, transient like a sand painting, and not the intellectual property (or theological gift) of a single person. At most, a few 5:00 p.m. preachers allowed the wondering questions they asked to catalyze responses by the assembly to be posted to one of the evening community's Facebook pages. Clearly, I transgress those earlier norms throughout this book by publishing six evening sermons, even if I am careful to label them "Remarks for Shared Homily" in square brackets. Their titles were also composed after the fact.

There's yet a more consequential creative tension between the verbal and the nonverbal woven into preaching at St. Paul's. The sermon is never the last word at any of the Sunday masses. And the last word is not really a word anyway. Preaching is always followed by eucharistic feasting. Both upstairs and downstairs, morning and evening, the community first *gathers* ritually in the Triune name of God. Then there is a service of the *word* in which Scripture is read, opened up, and applied to life through the sermon or shared homily; and the church confesses its faith, offers its prayers, and passes the peace of Christ among its members. Followed by a *meal*: bread and wine are taken, blessed, broken and poured out, shared. Finally, the community is *sent* out in mission, to work compassion and justice in the world. Hence, preaching is situated somewhere toward the middle of what is only the second of four movements in the symphony of Sunday worship, the second of four acts in its drama. Word, aurality and orality, need not carry all the weight—encompassed about as word always is by sight and touch and taste and smell, by gesture and symbol and silence and mystery.

Baby Sophia

Of course, St. Paul's is more than a building and its various rooms. More than a pulpit and a parish hall, worship services and sermons. As Gordon Lathrop insists, the primary liturgical reality is always the assembly itself. Church is people.[9]

Across the year bounded by the First Sunday of Advent 2016 and the Saturday following the Feast of Christ the King 2017, people were born at St. Paul's. People died. Old and young. Expectedly and unexpectedly. After many years of belonging, people moved away to other parts of the region and country and world. New people moved in and joined the parish community. People lost jobs. People took new jobs. People started school. People retired. People married. People split up. There were sorrows and joys. Triumphs and tragedies. And as an organization, an organism, the parish lived another year of its life. New leadership settled in. New resources became available. New needs emerged. Old strengths were nourished. Old institutional and interpersonal wounds persisted, even as other estrangements were overcome. As extreme shorthand for all things to do with the people of St. Paul's—shorthand for the context parish life provided for my year of preaching—I inscribe: *baby Sophia*.

Sophia's parents were active members of the 5:00 p.m. Sunday worshipping community. Sophia was their first child. Sophia, it was diagnosed during the first trimester of her gestation, carried the rare chromosomal anomaly trisomy 18. Instead of a normal pair, an extra chromosome 18 (a triple) disrupts the baby's normal pattern of development in significant, life-threatening ways, even before birth. Only 10 percent of infants with trisomy 18 survive to their first birthdays. Many are stillborn during the second or third trimesters of pregnancy.[10]

---

9. This central claim is already made in the first volume of his trilogy, Lathrop, *Holy Things*, especially 1–11 and 87–88; then greatly expanded, deepened, and applied in *Holy People*.

10. Information provided by the Trisomy 18 Foundation; see https://www.trisomy18.org.

Introduction

Baby Sophia's parents wrote these words for the worship bulletin provided at her requiem mass on May 5, 2017, after she died stillborn on April 28. "We felt it important early on after the diagnosis of trisomy 18 to name our little girl. We did not know how long she would be with us. 'Any day her heart could stop' . . . 'Trisomy 18 affects every cell' . . . 'We don't know if she can survive birth.' We heard this at every doctor's appointment, but we wanted to continue to hope that we would meet our little girl. So, we named her." Named her *Sophia*, because "it means Wisdom. [Because] in Feminist Christian theology this can be an image/word for the Spirit and/or Mystery of God." Because, Sophia's parents continued: "We hoped to be transformed by her and by this experience in ways that grew us closer to each other and to God. We knew we would need wisdom to navigate this journey and make what decisions were asked of us. And, the future at that point was a mystery to us."

So, for months, Sophia came to worship at St. Paul's in her mother's womb. We prayed for her by name each Sunday evening. Baby Sophia. She lived among us for a time. Then she died. Stillborn. We celebrated her life and commended her to God and committed her ashes to the earth in the Bolster Memorial Garden. Mother Sara Fischer preached the homily at baby Sophia's requiem mass. I was scheduled to preach on Sunday morning a couple of weeks later. The spark for that sermon of mine, "To an Unknown God in Whom We Live and Move and Have Our Being," came from some of Mother Sara's words and a breathtaking theological-spiritual insight they generated. More, later, in relation to the sixth sermon in the series, the one for the Sixth Sunday of Easter (May 21, 2017).

Donald Trump

Another context beyond the confines of the parish must loom large in any accounting of my year of occasional preaching: the uptown (or Lower Queen Anne) neighborhood where St. Paul's is located; the city of Seattle and King County and greater Puget Sound region; the state of Washington; the Pacific Northwest and entire West Coast; the United States, Western Hemisphere, and world. I'm referring to the social, political, and economic context. News and movies. Elections and movements. What a turbulent and supersaturated year it was! As cipher for the twelve months trailing back from early December 2017 to late November 2016, I pose the presidency of Donald J. Trump, although the context of these sermons was both more global and more local. Nevertheless, *Donald Trump*. And all the other issues implicated in and explicated by his election. ISIS. Iraq. Syria. Refugees and displaced people around the globe. Immigrants, asylum seekers, at the southern border of the United States. Sexual violence against women. Race in America. Disparities of wealth and privilege and access. The list could go on for as many pages as there are days in the year.

Locally, a driving social, political, and economic issue was housing in all its dimensions. We were told that in 2016–2017 Seattle was the fastest growing city in the U.S., with more people moving here than anywhere else—much of that influx because of the region's technology industry. Amazon. Microsoft. Google. And all the many, many ancillary businesses. On any given day, if you looked around the Seattle skyline, you would see dozens of construction cranes building both commercial and residential properties. But the tech boom and its construction boom made those new apartments and condos and retail spaces less and less affordable for all but highly paid newcomers and well-capitalized corporate entities. And, of course, rents in older buildings skyrocketed. Immigrant communities in the city of Seattle and historically African American neighborhoods were significantly emptied of those folk by aggressive gentrification and an exodus to suburbs like Renton and Kent. The block on which I live in Seattle had become much less diverse racially and ethnically, and in terms of age of residents, than it was a decade and a half earlier. Much more monocultural in terms of income level and type of employment. The color of my city was changing rapidly, as was its economic vibe. I found it hard to imagine the bus driver being able to afford to live in Seattle as I do. Or the checkout person at the grocery store. The men who pick up my garbage, compostable yard waste, and clean recycling. Or the women who make coffee for me or pull pints at the neighborhood pub. Indeed, my wife and I could not afford to purchase our own home now; prices have increased that much since 2002.

Linked to the above, but also with deep taproots in long unaddressed social issues, was the visible explosion of people living chronically unsheltered in Seattle, on the streets, in numerous large and small encampments—under bridges, beside highways, or on the sidewalk just outside of St. Paul's. This face of homelessness often manifests severe mental illness, substance abuse (and drug dealing), and/or physical disability—which made it all the more unsettling to learn that many of Seattle's new luxury condos sit permanently unoccupied, purchased solely as investments; to observe the house next door become an Airbnb helping to pay the mortgage on an additional home in Seattle, while some people have no home at all.

Introduction

If a primary local social/political/economic issue had to do with housing, then during 2016–2017, it became increasingly obvious to members of St. Paul's parish that whatever else we had at our disposal, we possessed and managed a house (the church building). Could we use our communal *house* to provide a surrogate *home* of various sorts to more of our immediate neighbors? (The word *oikos* in the Greek Testament of Christian Scripture refers both to the building and to the webs of human relationship and interaction housed there.) A monthly sit-down dinner for anyone and everyone, the Fatted Calf Café, continued to be served by St. Paul's during my year of occasional preaching. A mental health chaplaincy outpost moved to St. Paul's to offer direct services for those living unsheltered, as well as companionship training for members of the parish. A weekly arts program for unhoused folk began (first called the Karen Korn Project, since renamed Art Heals), as did a seven-day-a-week overnight shelter for women, in collaboration with a pair of not-for-profits, SHARE and WHEEL. And so, by the time I preached the twelfth sermon in this series—facilitating the shared homily on November 17, 2017—ten women had begun sleeping on mats on the floor of the parish hall where the altar sits on Sundays for the 5:00 p.m. mass—the same autumn when a significant number of individuals, couples, and family units from the 5:00 p.m. worshipping community moved out of Seattle (and away from active participation at St. Paul's) in order to find affordable housing, including baby Sophia's parents.

In addition to being one of the preachers at St. Paul's during the 2016–2017 church year, I served on the vestry (elected by the congregation) and as senior warden (appointed by the rector). For those of you not fluent in Episcopal-ese (and why should you be?), the vestry is the governing body of lay leaders of a congregation: the church board or session. The senior warden works alongside the rector, overseeing vestry work and congregational life, and serves as advisor to the rector. Neither role is directly related to preaching. But being senior warden did mean I was responsible for giving a report at the February 4, 2018, annual meeting of the parish. And because I also happened to be scheduled to preach at the three masses that morning, I chose to offer my senior warden's report in the form of a word cloud, just to spare people from having to listen to my voice on and off from 7:30 a.m. until 2:00 p.m. Some of my *written* words tried to catch up the national context of the year just past (for example, RESISTANCE and Dumbfounded). Others, the local social, political, and economic situation (UPZONING, Encampments, and DISLOCATION). Still others what was

So Fill Our Imaginations

going on within the parish community itself (DEPARTURES and SHELTER, Reach and resilience). Some of these words receive comment later in connection with particular sermons. At this point, I hope they provide a wide-angle snapshot of contexts. The shape containing the word cloud traces the roofline and Roy Street front of St. Paul's 1963 building.

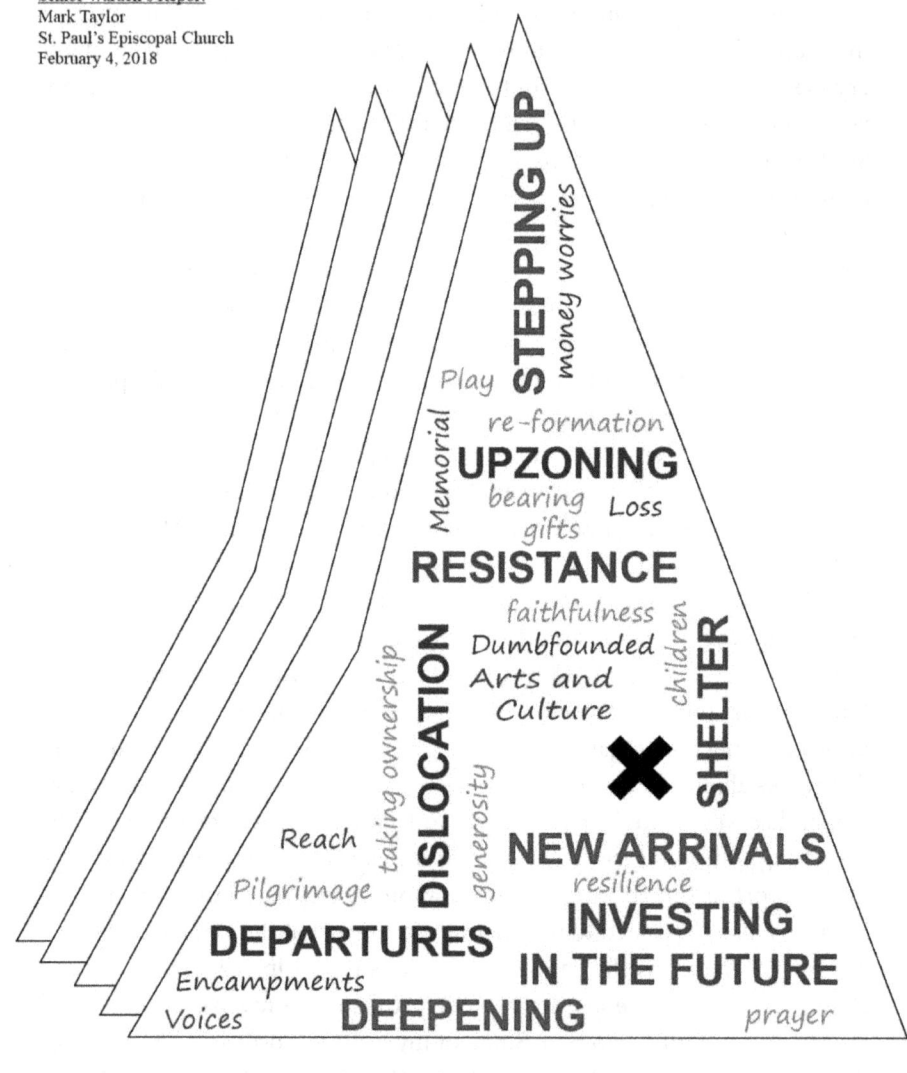

Senior Warden's Report
Mark Taylor
St. Paul's Episcopal Church
February 4, 2018

Social/Political/Economic Context

Introduction

Lectionary Year A

A note about the texts in front of this preacher as he composed and delivered these twelve sermons. St. Paul's uses the Revised Common Lectionary (RCL) as source for its Sunday Scripture readings. Some of you will recognize in my sermons that after several three-year cycles following track 1 of the RCL for our first reading during the long season after Pentecost (the one with semicontinuous readings of the Hebrew patriarchal/matriarchal stories during Year A; the saga of the house of David and Jerusalem and the temple in Year B; and then, for Year C, the prophets of Israel), St. Paul's reverted to track 2, the older set of first readings cued by some link to the Gospel for the day, resonant or contrasting.

The 2016–2017 church year was *Lectionary Year A*. The year in the cycle that leans into the Gospel of Matthew. I confess to you, my siblings, to the Blessed Virgin Mary, Blessed Paul, Blessed Benedict, Blessed Mary Magdalene, Blessed Julian of Norwich, . . . and all the saints, that Matthew is not my favorite Gospel. I know that says more about me, my social location and context, than about Matthew. But still, it's true. I gravitate more naturally to Jesus the rebel in the Gospel of Mark, or Jesus the mystic in John, than to Matthew with his rabbi Jesus.[11] The stumbling blocks and millstones are indeed hard and heavy for me, as are those sayings about separations—weeds from wheat, sheep from goats. All that weeping and gnashing of teeth in outer darkness. So, twelve months of occasional preaching during Lectionary Year A forced upon me the opportunity of wrestling with Matthew. To try to listen more deeply to Matthew and the realities of Matthew's community. To listen to others talk about Matthew today. In the course on Jesus the Christ I teach at school, I encourage my students to notice—as we work through New Testament Christologies—which of the four Gospel portraits of Jesus most appeals to them and which they find immediately most repellent or challenging. I encourage them to sit intentionally with that problematic Gospel. I had to take my own exercise to heart and put it into practice, with respect to Matthew, over the twelve months in and around these twelve sermons. Although it would be helpful if the saying were found in Matthew's Gospel, nonetheless, I cite Luke 4:23: "Doctor, cure yourself!"

For six years, I served as director of worship for the School of Theology and Ministry. You should know that the average age of our students is

---

11. See Griffith-Jones, *Four Witnesses*.

somewhere north of forty-two. Mature adults! They personally represent the school's diversity of ecclesial partners: Roman Catholic layfolk, as well as people headed toward lay and ordained ministries in the Episcopal, Lutheran, Presbyterian, United Methodist churches, and the United Church of Christ; Baptists, Mennonites, Unitarian Universalists, white Evangelicals, and black church folk, including Pentecostals. Many have been active in their congregations for years. All are required to do field work or contextual education in internship sites—many in parishes. So, some of my students are themselves honing skills for preaching and nurturing a sustainable spirituality of preaching. One of my favorite programs as director of worship was hosting Tuesday brown bag lunches devoted to study and discussion of the coming Sunday's Scripture readings with an eye toward preaching them (even with students from non-lectionary traditions). As you will read later, these discussions have been formative for my own development as a preacher. For although these lunchtime gatherings were anchored in specific Scripture readings from the lectionary, they always set sail for what it might mean to preach in all our various congregational contexts and what it might mean for us all to be church today (locally, ecumenically, and globally). I wonder if you regular preachers among my readers are privileged to have a community of challenge and support such as this for your preaching? If not, consider seeking one out or convening one!

Now, I sincerely hope that there are folk from non-lectionary traditions among the readers of this book. You may already be wondering about the impact of the lectionary on how these sermons were crafted. First of all, let me say, I believe preachers from lectionary and non-lectionary traditions have much to learn from each other. So, let's talk. I am grateful for the gift of being part of such conversations first hand, not only during the Tuesday brown bag lunches just mentioned but also in my basic worship and beginning preaching classes at school, where half of my students have been Unitarian Universalists, along with free church Protestants and black church worship leaders and preachers, all without commitment to a lectionary of any sort; the other half—Roman Catholic, Episcopal, Lutheran, Presbyterian students, and so on—much more likely to shape Sunday preaching and worship around a lectionary-driven set of authorized Scripture readings. Let's keep talking, for these traditions would seem to nurture very different processes of sermon composition. Maybe? For, on the other hand, I suspect there might be a deeper commonality between

Introduction

the two traditions. Doesn't preaching, with or without a lectionary, require the preacher to stage a dialogue between the wisdom of their religious heritage(s), including Scripture(s), and the experience(s), the situation(s), of their listeners and communities here and now?

My opening remarks in a conversation between people from different preaching traditions would include the following. The lectionary, with its three Scripture readings and psalm appointed for each Sunday and other holy day on the calendar of the church year, certainly does *constrain* me as preacher. These texts—and not others—will be read or sung or chanted immediately before any and every sermon at St. Paul's. Preaching thereby defaults to being biblical, rather than thematic. In Lectionary Year A, for example, the Gospel of Matthew will set the tone, one way or another, much of the time. Not everything will be possible, or easy, for the preacher to say on a given Sunday. However, I would hasten to add that the lectionary can also *cajole* the preacher to be more creative, more imaginative. The lectionary can free the preacher from the morass of too many decisions to make. The biblical texts appointed by the lectionary provide a foundation, a center, an antidote to the dizziness of possibility—a stable, built-in dialogue partner or sounding board. A convenient launch or landing for a sermon. I don't know much about weaving as an artform, but how about this image: the lectionary's Scripture readings represent the fixed warp for a sermon, with everything else brought by preacher and congregation and community and nation and world the weft plied in and out by a homiletical shuttle to complete the full fabric?[12]

Enough about texts and contexts. To my year of preaching and the twelve sermons themselves—their composition and delivery, reception and subsequent agency. Travel back with me to December 2016: Advent and preparation for celebrating the birth of Christ Jesus. Opening up Matthew's Gospel. First, paging toward the end to an apocalyptic warning: "If the owner of the house had known in what part of the night the thief was coming, [they] would have stayed awake and would not have let [their] house be broken into. Therefore you also must be ready" (Matt 24:43–44 on the First Sunday of Advent). Then back to the beginning and the infancy narrative (Matt 1:18–25, Fourth Sunday). After the election of Donald Trump as

---

12. There are lots of books out there on preaching. I mean a lot. Really. A lot! And here I'm adding one more. In my beginning preaching class with students equally divided between lectionary and non-lectionary traditions, I require two textbooks, one representing each approach, and every student must read both, regardless of their tradition. See Hogan, *Graceful Speech*, and Rzepka and Sawyer, *Thematic Preaching*.

president of the United States, but before his inauguration. And there, too, baby Sophia, several months old in her mother's womb, already afflicted with trisomy 18.

1

Seeing the Signs

The Fourth Sunday of Advent

THROUGHOUT THE REMAINDER OF this book, I will have commentary to offer both before and after each particular sermon and preaching occasion. In this first instance, however, all my reflections follow. Afterwards. As some afterwords.

"Seeing the Signs"
The Fourth Sunday of Advent
Isaiah 7:10–16; Psalm 80:1–7, 16–18; Romans 1:1–7; Matthew 1:18–25
December 18, 2016

"The LORD himself will give you a sign. Look, the young woman is with child and shall bear a son, and shall name him Immanuel [God is with us]."

—ISAIAH 7:14 [MATTHEW 1:23]

I used to be such a good navigator behind the steering wheel of a car. Given a map with enough detail, I could locate almost any address. Even a few lines drawn on a scrap of paper indicating key highways or cross streets most often led me to my destination. And I used to have an intuitive sense—without any map at all—of whether to turn left or right, drive up and over or around and across. GPS and Google maps and other technologies have changed all this. I have changed. I have developed quite a serious electronic dependency. Oh, I still get where I need to go. But following that bright arrow on the screen and listening to those synthesized, prerecorded voice commands, I am led passively, almost blindly. I fail to *see* the signs along the way, let alone *heed* them, signs that used to be vital in navigating.

༄ ༅

Ahaz and Joseph. Two men in this morning's Scripture readings who nearly failed to see the signs. Signs reading: "God is with us."

Ahaz was king of Judah when unprecedented political and military disaster befell his nation. The other Hebrew kingdom, Israel, turned against their siblings in Judah, entered into an unholy alliance with traditional adversary Aram, and attacked Jerusalem. Earlier in Isaiah 7, we are told that when "the house of David" learned of this alliance, "the heart of Ahaz and the heart of his people shook as the trees of the forest shake before the wind" (7:2). King Ahaz responds to this existential threat by blindly following the political and military GPS of his day. Ahaz connives his own unholy alliance with an even greater power—the Assyrian Empire, sending a huge treasure of gold and silver removed from the temple in Jerusalem as tribute, and rebuilding the Hebrew house of God to mimic an Assyrian temple in Damascus (2 Kgs 16).

Given Judah's fearful situation, you might think it would be *Ahaz* beseeching God for a sign. Just the reverse. In our first reading, *God* begs Ahaz to request a sign—one as potent as possible: "Ask a sign of the LORD your God; let it be as deep as the underworld or as high as heaven" (Isa 7:11). Ahaz refuses, locked up blind in his own schemes for national survival: "I will not ask, and I will not put the LORD to the test" (Isa 7:12). Well then, Isaiah replies, expressing God's weariness that the king would dismiss what God freely offers, which was just what Ahaz tried so frantically to accomplish through his political and military maneuvers: "Therefore the LORD himself will give you a sign. Look, the young woman is with child and shall bear a son, and shall name him Immanuel . . . . For before the child knows how to refuse the evil and choose the good, the land before whose two kings you are in dread will be deserted" (Isa 7:14, 16).

Immanuel. God is with us. Not an aggressive, masculine sign of conquest, but a feminine one like the moon's gentle, inexorable tug on the tides, or the cycle of the seasons—summer, followed by fall and winter, and only then spring. A domestic sign. A pregnant young woman. God is with us. Not a sign of distance or delay, that God will be with Judah later after they have shored things up politically and militarily. No, here and now, in fearful and unprecedented times, God is with us. Not a sign subject to a range of probabilities. Instead, a most urgent, unmistakable sign. The young woman *is* with child, very pregnant. The baby *is* on its way, with that heavy, downward movement. And you shall name him Immanuel, God is with us. A sign of new life, rather than defeat or an ending.

Joseph is a *righteous* man, our Gospel reading from Matthew tells us (Matt 1:19). Wide awake in the noonday brightness of conventional morality and social conformity. Following prerecorded voice commands, not just according to the letter of the law but also its deeper spirit. Then disaster strikes Joseph, as it did Ahaz. Joseph's may seem to be just a domestic emergency—but there are public consequences at stake, life-and-death ones. For Mary, the young woman to whom righteous Joseph is engaged to be married, turns out to be pregnant—and the child is not Joseph's! In a traditional society strictly controlling women's sexuality, Joseph quite literally has Mary's life in his hands. He has every right to pursue charges of promiscuous infidelity against her. Instead, amazingly, Joseph chooses to go way out on a limb and beyond all expectations. Unwilling to expose Mary to public disgrace, he resolves to dismiss her quietly. Joseph's moral and social GPS is functioning at its very best. The situation seems perfectly under control. As a man, Joseph has available to him the choice to separate from Mary and go on living without her. He cannot imagine a way for them to stay together, what with a child that is not his own. But *even* at his very best, *even* at his most righteous, *especially* at his best and most righteous, Joseph nearly fails to see the sign: God is with us.

Breaking into his masculine, noonday moral clarity comes an angel. In a dream. At night. "'Joseph, son of David, do not be afraid to take Mary as your wife, for the child conceived in her is from the Holy Spirit. She will bear a son, and you are to name him Jesus, for he will save his people from their sins.' All this took place to fulfill what had been spoken by the Lord through the prophet: 'Look, the virgin shall conceive and bear a son, and they shall name him Emmanuel,' which means 'God is with us'" (Matt 1:20–23). And so Joseph's life changes forever. To see and heed the sign—God is with us—Joseph must stay with the vulnerable young woman and marry her. Joseph must partner with Mary in parenting the child who

So Fill Our Imaginations

would otherwise have been orphaned. And Joseph must give the son who is not his own a name: Jesus. Emmanuel. God is with us.

※ ※

I wonder what angels appear to us, when all that we resolve to do in fearful and unprecedented times of disaster falls asleep—whether unholy alliances or righteous accomplishments? What nighttime dreams break into our noonday clarity? What feminine signs of emergence beckon *by way of* the darkness, not in spite of it? And where might the sign—God is with us—lead, anyway?

Words about "God in Disguise" from a blog post by a woman identified only as Lisa might help us begin to navigate these questions. Lisa writes, "In this season of Advent we continue to make our way through a broken, painful world. We are watching and waiting for Jesus but we can't make sense of the happenings around us. All the decorations and the signs that say we should be rejoicing seem pale in comparison to the news of the day. I drive by a colorful nativity scene on someone's front lawn and it seems so irrelevant. I hear the music *all is calm, all is bright* and I cringe.

"As I cleaned my house yesterday," Lisa continues, "I listened [on the radio] to . . . a love story between two very broken people who longed for hope. I saw their lament and their celebration. I was surprised at how alive I felt as I listened. Here is this expletive filled tale about a junkie and a prostitute. Here is a story of people on the fringe of society. Here is a story of life and death. Here is the story of AIDS and abandonment by friends. But yet! when he talks about Franny's last [motorcycle] ride and the wind on their faces—I could see God. As he explained the feeling of the hospice workers cheering them on and the last ride of freedom—I could feel God. As he talked about two people who life didn't know what to do with—I knew God.

"We want to keep our ideas and beliefs pure and separate from the ugliness of life. But what if that is exactly where God is? What if [God] really is in the messiest places? . . . I don't think it matters if you are a junkie or a prostitute; . . . that you are mad at the world; . . . that you are stuck in lament. I don't think it matters if you lose your cool with the kids; . . . if you can't find God in church. I don't think it matters how our life comes to us. I think God is in it, especially in those places we can barely see."

Lisa concludes: "Where could God be today? Has [God] come to you, disguised as life? These are the questions we hold as we move forward in this holiday season. Holding joy and lament, holding loss and life.

> Light a candle.
> Tell someone you love them.
> Forgive yourself.
> Be still.
> Find small glimpses of hope.
> Make a new friend.
> Carry the hard stuff together.
> Take that [motorcycle] ride and feel the wind on your face.
> God is here.
> Find [God's] disguise."

I am a vocational theologian. I teach regularly—day after day, year in and year out—in an academic context, a university school of theology and ministry. I preach only occasionally.

Where did my theological vocation come from? Ultimately, it has something to do with being raised in a family and by parents who were equal parts, genuinely and fully, scientific, artistic, and pious. My dad is a retired chemistry professor. On our family walks in the Blue Hills outside Boston on Sunday afternoons, he instilled in us curiosity about the natural world, and wonder. What is that? Sassafras tree. A gall on an oak. Flicker. Why does it look like that? Grow there? Have such long feet and toes? My mom played piano, and my dad sang bass. By the time I was twelve or so, I knew Handel's *Messiah* by heart, having heard the college's choral union perform it every December. Our family belonged to and actively worshipped within the Church of the Nazarene, one of the fruits of the late-nineteenth-early-twentieth-century American holiness movement. But I experienced the Church of the Nazarene in communities surrounding one or another of its liberal arts colleges. First of all, the one in New England (Eastern Nazarene College). Unlike some of my peers, I did not receive this tradition in its legalistic form. Instead, my Christian formation centered around friendship with Jesus and the mysterious workings of a powerful Holy Spirit. Science. The arts. Piety. Not a bad combination for any child. One that steered me first toward an interest in paleontology in high school—until I wrote my senior project on the political ideals in Plato's *Republic*. Then to a philosophy major in college—until those classes on Kierkegaard and existentialism and the philosophy of religion. And so to graduate studies in theology and a subsequent teaching career.

Every preacher, like every religious educator or pastoral counselor or faith-based community activist, always already has an operative theology within them out of which their ministry comes. This is no less, no more, true of me. It's just that to teach theology to other people, to try and facilitate their theological reflection, I have been forced to be more explicit about my own theologizing. I have needed to be able to come clean on how and with what resources I do theology, in order—with all due respect—to require my students to identify and examine, maybe deconstruct and reconstruct, their theologies. And so a set of core convictions about God, the universe, human communities and institutions and persons, functions behind and beneath my preaching, as expressed in these twelve sermons. I wonder, by the *end* of our shared journey through a year of preaching, how you might describe my operative theology. And I wonder if the piecemeal account of my theological journey might also help the reader identify their own.

Here at the *beginning*, I want to lift up just two indispensable resources for my theologizing as I understand it: the resources offered by feminist and womanist theology, and those of the process theologians. Or, formulated as a pair of convictions, how about:

1. Women are fully human. And, the full humanity of women can never simply be taken for granted; it must be secured, expanded, protected socially/politically/economically, everywhere and everywhen. But, there is no *one* such thing as women's experience; it is always incarnated in and complicated by race and culture and class—which behooves me, as a white man, to attend to the particularly crucial and critical vantage point occupied by women *of color*.

2. God is *most*, not *least*, related to other beings, *all* other beings. The universe, any and all universes, exist within the encompassing reality of God. Hence, the God-world relationship is better thought of in terms of metaphors of spirit animating a universal body than a cosmic artisan fashioning something.

I'll discuss the former conviction here, the latter in the orienting remarks for the sixth of these sermons.

Seeing the Signs

Some of you may already find it problematic that I refer to feminist *and* womanist theology as *one* of my indispensable resources. *Feminist* and *womanist* are very different, you may be thinking. I agree. Hang in there with me, please, as I develop this topic. I do not mean to equate feminist and womanist theologies with my *and*, although I do want to connect them when I reflect upon my own education and formation. For the direction, the vector, of the raising of my social/political/economic consciousness has in fact been from gender and sex to race.

I remember exactly when I heard the word *feminism* for the first time. It was 1969. I was a junior in high school, and my classmate Ann used it. I did not know what the word meant and had to ask her, "What is feminism?" Ann said something to the effect of: "It's like the struggle for civil rights, only for women." (Need I say, Ann and I were both white?) Oh, I replied. Okay, that makes sense. Over the next decade and a half, the consistent presence and pressure of many, many women helped feminism make more and more sense to my life in the world, my theological vocation, and my faith.

Two strong, gifted daughters formed my identity as parent. It seems likely that in the late 1970s, I was among the first generation of male seminarians and PhD students gifted with classrooms that more or less resembled the general population of the United States—just over half female. In graduate school, I read Mary Daly and Rosemary Radford Ruether.[1] Early in my teaching career, the ecofeminist work of Sallie McFague became pivotal, as did books by medieval mystics Catherine of Siena and Margery Kempe (Kempe was introduced to me, fittingly enough, by a female student) and by historian Caroline Walker Bynum.[2] From the beginning, the undergraduate and graduate programs in which I taught were always more like 75 percent female students, 25 percent male. And the federated United Church of Christ/Presbyterian Church (USA) congregation my daughters, their mother, and I attended those days in Boston had two women (and an African American man) on a clergy staff of four! Two female ministers preaching, teaching, giving pastoral care, baptizing, officiating at the Lord's Supper.

Then, in the mid-1980s, I read Alice Walker's *The Color Purple*. In my opinion, one of the greatest novels of the twentieth century. A work of art

---

1. Daly, *Beyond God the Father* and *Gyn/Ecology*; Ruether, *Sexism and God-Talk*.
2. McFague, *Models of God*; Catherine of Siena, *Dialogue*; Kempe, *Book of Margery Kempe*; Bynum, *Holy Feast and Holy Fast*.

that incubated perfectly a developing feature of my college classrooms: to teach theology by engaging religious or spiritual themes in literature and film, painting and music. ("God in Human Experience" is a rubric I use to name this feature.) I still know of no other novel that shows how inextricably connected self-image and image of God can be in a person's life, how intertwined the human body, the social body, and spirit (human and divine). I continue to be privileged to teach *The Color Purple* every other academic year.

Alice Walker gets credit for coining the term *womanist*. Her classic four-part definition derives womanist from the African American colloquial expression *womanish*, which means being grown up, responsible, in charge (the opposite of girlish, or frivolous, irresponsible, not serious), and includes a woman who loves other women, sexually and/or nonsexually, and who also loves music, dance, the moon, the Spirit, love and food and roundness, . . . loves herself. *Regardless*.[3] Which encouraged me to explore the work of several womanist theologians, above all, Delores Williams and her book *Sisters in the Wilderness*, which soon showed up as required reading in one of my courses.[4] Something in the theology of these black women resonated more deeply with the spirituality of my holiness roots than had white feminist theology. And shifted my theological method by making the experience pole of the dialogue with tradition both more complex and more properly reflective of the world's people—exposing my white privilege, substantively, for the first time and beckoning me to begin to learn to use my social location as an ally of and with *black folk*, in addition to women.

So, this vocational theologian and occasional preacher—with some trepidation and sincere confessions of inadequacy—will say he aspires to be a feminist theologian—a white, male, feminist theologian—who appreciates, in the words of Alice Walker's definition again, that *womanist* is to feminist as *purple* is to lavender. Purple has always been my favorite color.

By the 1990s and 2000s, I felt challenged in my scholarly research to try to read with and against the grain of the writings of two nineteenth-century male authors: Herman Melville and Søren Kierkegaard—teasing out their constructions of gender, the possibilities and cul-de-sacs therein. Instead of presuming to speak *for* women, maybe I could assist the cause a little by speaking to and about men, white men, and our ways—liberating

---

3. Walker, *In Search*, xi–xii.

4. See also Grant, *White Women's Christ*; Douglas, *Black Christ*; and Hayes, *Hagar's Daughters*.

and not so much—of bringing experience together with the Christian tradition.[5] Both Melville and Kierkegaard will make cameo appearances in this book.

Let me now close the loop from actual women face to face and side by side in my life to books by female writers and back again. I treasure all that I have learned from women colleagues and students, colleagues and students of color, at school, at church, in my academic guilds. Including, at long last for me, from transgender folk—black and white—and theologies and spiritualities that queer it all, making exclusive binaries (beginning with male and female) seem quaint and constricting. One small testimony to this is my attempt to use pronouns *they/them/their* to refer to people throughout this book, except where I know otherwise explicitly from the person her- or himself.

Almost no matter what the Scripture readings in front of me, I'm drawn to try and preach the great reversals of the gospel of Jesus Christ. Reversals of the sort proclaimed, for example, in Luke 14 and appointed by the common lectionary for reading on the Twelfth Sunday after Pentecost, Year C: "When you are invited by someone to a wedding banquet, do not sit down at the place of honor, in case someone more distinguished than you has been invited by your host; . . . . But when you are invited, go and sit down at the lowest place, so that when your host comes [they] may say to you, 'Friend, move up higher'; then you will be honored in the presence of all who sit at the table with you. For all who exalt themselves will be humbled, and those who humble themselves will be exalted" (Luke 14:8, 10–11). I often use the language of turning things upside down and inside out to characterize the sayings and doings of Jesus—his upsetting of hierarchies. But I'm learning from wise women and people of color and queer folk to be cautious around constructs like higher/lower, up/down, center/at the margins, humble/exalted, lest they become construed as exclusive binaries. Suspicious that while for some human beings—the privileged, like me—a sinful missing of the mark may indeed take the form of pride or too *much* self, for others, the path away from being who God made them to be is precisely persistent, imposed self-negation, too *little* self, within the structures of society/politics/economics. And so, for the latter person, the call to humble themself represents the opposite of liberation, of good news. Instead, rise up and become fully who you already truly are.

---

5. M. L. Taylor, "Ishmael's (m)Other"; "Almost Earnestness"; "Practice in Authority"; "Well-Considered Occasion"; and "Hermit Emerges Victorious."

So Fill Our Imaginations

Which is why I have also tried to leverage texts like John 13–15 where Jesus begins by marking out his relationship to his disciples in terms of the binary: master and servant (okay, let's be more honest than the NRSV to the Greek *doulos*, "slave"), but makes it clear his work is not to replace one set of human masters with another, the former slaves, keeping a one up/one down binary in place, but instead to remake both master and slave as something, someone else—friends, inaugurating a new humanity of beloved ones.[6] Now, masters and slaves do not become beloved ones in the same way. Masters are recreated as beloved ones by learning to serve others in love; slaves, by taking their rightful place as fully human beings free from enslavement to any human master. It may be that only the witness of the slave can free the master to hear the gospel not as an ideological sanction for their own privilege, but as the good news of God's love for all. And yet, I'm coming to realize that this theological and spiritual move of mine needs to become more and more intersectional today, concretized by race in America and queered, at the same time.

I hope an appropriate and non-appropriating use of the resources of feminist and womanist theologies characterizes my preaching. In preparing for the preceding sermon, the first of the twelve, I heard in the Gospel reading (Matt 1:18–25) the incipient dismantling of another binary, that of light and darkness. Here, evangelical transformation takes place by way of darkness, not in spite of it or by avoiding it. Surely the easier response for Joseph—when he hears the news that Mary, his betrothed, is pregnant—would have been to break with her over the principle of the thing, as Carol Gilligan has said typifies Western male moral development.[7] Harder, more costly, for Joseph to hang in there, to stay in relationship with Mary and the child-to-be. The socially/politically/economically more transgressive breach turns out not to be a break at all but deeper connection. Barbara Brown Taylor makes a similar move not to valorize the light of abstract principle over against the fraught darkness of real relationship in her book *Learning to Walk in the Dark*, which I heard her speak about at my university a year or so after I had composed and delivered "Seeing the Signs." She spoke of God doing some of God's best work at night. Some of God's best *play* at night, I wonder? And I'm coming to realize that these moves by Carol Gilligan and Mark Lloyd Taylor and Barbara Brown Taylor need to become more and more intersectional today. Concretized by race in

---

6. M. L. Taylor, "Boundless Love of God," 138.
7. Gilligan, *In a Different Voice*.

America. Thank you, Delores Williams, for your devastating, self- and worldview-altering exposé of the social/political/economic construction of the colors white (good and pure: everything from angel food cake to "wash me whiter than snow, Lord, whiter than snow") and black (soiled and evil: blackmail, blackballing, blacklisted, and so on).[8] And queered at the same time. Rendering and reframing and reclaiming my use of masculine/feminine language in the foregoing sermon as tactical and contextual, rather than essentializing.

One final thought, which probably calls for another book entirely. I'm not sure I could write it, however. It feels simultaneously presumptuous and inadequate. But here it goes. There's a corner of my social location, and so of my vocation, where the resources of feminist and womanist theologies dovetail with a thrice-repeated discernment on my part *not* to pursue ordination, to forego at least that one position of power available to me. Throughout my teaching career, I have had to correct students, colleagues, and constituents who, in addition to the *Doctor* that appropriately precedes my name, have bestowed upon me the titles *Reverend* or *Father* Taylor. Early on, in Church of the Nazarene contexts, many people found it unintelligible that I could function as a theologian without having been ordained a pastor. Over the past twenty-five years at Seattle University, my status as a lay theologian has placed me in solidarity with Roman Catholic women, while setting me apart a little from the ordained folk in Anglican, Protestant, and Unitarian communities I also engage on a daily basis. Within the Episcopal Church and St. Paul's parish, my anomalous standpoint sometimes nudges me, respectfully and with self-deprecating humor, to point out that that white robe, that alb, worn by the layperson who carries the processional cross or swings the thurible during the liturgy, is the same garment the deacon wears under their dalmatic and stole, the priest under cope or chasuble, the bishop along with miter and crozier, because the alb is our common, baptismal vestment. My fantasy would be for every member of the congregation to be given an alb at the door of the church, by the baptismal font, and wear it throughout the mass. For *liturgy* means the work, the public works, of the people. (Today, we might interrogate whether the common baptismal garment should be white!) All this to say, theologizing—including the

---

8. D. Williams, ch. 4, "Color Struck: A State of Mind," in *Sisters*, 84–107. In his recent book, *Dear Church*, Lenny Duncan offers alternatives to the whiteness of much traditional Christian language and imagery.

work and play of preaching—roots itself in baptismal identity, however much ordination sets a few of the baptized apart and clothes them for specific functions around word and sacrament within the church.

2

Walking Makes the Way
The Third Sunday after the Epiphany

My second sermon of the church year overtly brought together national news, the life of the parish, and the Gospel of Matthew all at once. The word *inaugurations* provided a conceptual through line, while *walking* gave that idea metaphorical legs. This particular sermon, however, requires some background reflection on how politics and preaching tend to intersect at St. Paul's.

The pulpit in the upstairs worship space at St. Paul's, whence I delivered this Sunday morning sermon, was designed and built by Cornish College of the Arts Professor John Gierlich and replaced one original to the 1963 building. Gierlich's pulpit forms a kind of blunt-faced triangle pointing toward the congregation, made up of five enameled metal panels mounted in a wooden superstructure. The panels are blue, with black and pale blue tracery and figures and designs. Lots of circles with crosses and eight-pointed stars. Birds—mostly crows. Plant life. The front panel features a large vessel, an amphora, upright, but with water flowing up and out in all directions—or vines, rather, growing every which way. According to the artist, this represents proclamation as a source of the water of life. A smaller pitcher on one of the side panels mirrors this theme. Such symbols can also be found in the sage-green metal fencing surrounding the St. Paul's property, which was executed earlier by another local artist, Deborah Mersky.[1] Inside the pulpit—which only the preacher and a few other altar

---

1. St. Paul's has prepared a booklet on *Art around the Parish*; see p. 2 for discussion of

So Fill Our Imaginations

servers can see during mass—is a beautiful assemblage of delicate wooden ribs and sheathing. So, as I maintained earlier, more than anything else, this pulpit resembles the prow of a ship.

Whenever I step up into the St. Paul's pulpit, I recall a series of three chapters from Herman Melville's *Moby-Dick*.[2] As he waits to set out on his nineteenth-century whaling voyage, Ishmael, narrator of the book, finds himself in New Bedford, Massachusetts, where he takes time to visit a famous church—frequented by whalemen and their families and pastored by one Father Mapple who himself was a whaler earlier in life. Ishmael first describes the chapel. Then he remarks how nautical its pulpit was, to the extent, even, that the preacher could enter it only by climbing up a rope ladder (which was then hauled inside). The prow of a ship, visually and practically. But as so often happens, Ishmael is led by physical appearance and function to muse upon deeper spiritual truths.

> What could be more full of meaning?—for the pulpit is ever this earth's foremost part; all the rest comes in its rear; the pulpit leads the world. From thence it is the storm of God's quick wrath is first descried, and the bow must bear the earliest brunt. From thence it is the God of breezes fair or foul is first invoked for favorable winds. Yes, the world's a ship on its passage out, and not a voyage complete; and the pulpit is its prow.[3]

Ishmael finds these musings reinforced in the sermon he hears Father Mapple preach that day. Appropriately, Mapple chooses to preach on the book of Jonah, a whale of a story from the Hebrew Testament of Christian Scripture. He delivers what he styles "a two-stranded lesson": one "to all us sinful [people]"[4] and a second specifically to Mapple himself as "pilot of the living God."[5] The more universal lesson amounts to: "Sin not; but if you do, take heed to repent of it like Jonah."[6] I've always found the other lesson more intriguing, the demand directed to the "anointed pilot-prophet"— Mapple or Jonah or any other preacher—"To preach the Truth to the face of Falsehood!"[7] And "woe to that pilot of the living God," Mapple says,

---

the ambo/pulpit and p. 3 for the fence.
2. Melville, *Moby-Dick*, chs. 7, 8, and 9.
3. Melville, *Moby-Dick*, 43–44.
4. Melville, *Moby-Dick*, 45.
5. Melville, *Moby-Dick*, 50.
6. Melville, *Moby-Dick*, 49.
7. Melville, *Moby-Dick*, 50.

"who slights" this demand. Woe to the one "whom this world charms from Gospel duty"; "who seeks to pour oil upon the waters when God has brewed them into a gale"; "who seeks to please rather than to appall"; "whose good name is more to [them] than goodness"; "who, in this world, courts not dishonor!" "Yea, woe to [the one] who, as the great Pilot Paul has it, while preaching to others is [themself] a castaway [1 Cor 9:27]!"[8]

Instead of woe, however, Mapple closes the sermon with "deep joy in his eyes, as he cried out with a heavenly enthusiasm" and—more relevant for us here—as he also charts a passage through faith and American politics and preaching:

> But oh! shipmates! on the starboard hand of every woe, there is a sure delight; and higher the top of that delight, than the bottom of the woe is deep . . . . Delight is to [the one]—a far, far upward, and inward delight—who against the proud gods and commodores of this earth, ever stands forth [their] own inexorable self . . . . Who gives no quarter in the truth, and kills, burns, and destroys all sin though [they] pluck it out from under the robes of Senators and Judges. Delight,—top-gallant delight is to [the one], who acknowledges no law or lord, but the Lord [their] God, *and is only a patriot to heaven*.[9]

Now, Father Mapple's sermon resonates with its own distinctive mid-nineteenth-century New England/New York political and religious context and with Melville's complex dialogue with the deepest values of the Dutch Calvinist heritage of his mother Maria Gansevoort and those of his father Allan Melvill's Unitarianism (the *e* was added to the family name after the father's death). A much different context for preaching, surely, than at St. Paul's Episcopal Church, Seattle, Washington in 2016–2017? Nevertheless, I find Mapple's sermon still relevant, at least in raising the question of what it means to preach the gospel in America. If not more, for Herman Melville's narrator imagines the "Whaling Voyage by One Ishmael" sandwiched between two and only two other items on the playbill of Providence: a "Grand Contested Election for the Presidency of the United States" and "Bloody Battle in Afghanistan"—uncanny, right?[10]

8. Melville, *Moby-Dick*, 50.

9. Melville, *Moby-Dick*, 50–51 (emphasis added).

10. Melville, *Moby-Dick*, 16. My favorite teacher at Mount Vernon Senior High School (Mount Vernon, Ohio) was Evelyn Roeder, who taught American literature. Her class introduced me to *Moby-Dick*, and I wrote a paper (immodestly for a sixteen-year-old high school junior) on "*the* biblical allusions" in Melville's novel. That paper birthed

So Fill Our Imaginations

I hope my occasional preaching offers some gift to the regular preachers at St. Paul's beyond a Sunday morning or evening off. Although maybe that would be gift enough in a parish with as many Sunday liturgies as St. Paul's, to say nothing of weekday services. Whether or not our clergy would see it this way, I have always perceived my preaching as an attempt to fill in an empty space or explore a corner or offer a bit of contrast or shading to their sermons. So, I took my cues on how to preach during the first months of the presidency of Donald J. Trump from our rector, Sara Fischer. Two examples of how she engaged politics in her preaching.

Sara preached at the Sunday morning masses on October 16, 2016—during the last month of the presidential election campaign and a little over a week after the release of the *Access Hollywood* tape in which Donald Trump described and boasted of kissing women uninvited and "grab[bing] them by the pussy. You can do anything you want."[11] Sara never referred to the tape explicitly or named Trump directly. Instead, her sermon "Living Inside Out and Outside In" weaves together the story of Jacob and Esau (Gen 32:22–31) and Parker Palmer's use of a mobius strip to talk about human identity. The mobius is a strip of paper that can be joined into a circle (still with two separate sides along which you could run a finger) or twisted with the ends held together in a figure-eight shape—one in which, mysteriously, "if you move your finger around it, inside becomes outside and outside becomes inside."[12] Here's how Sara sought to open up the story of Jacob using Palmer's mobius strip (and to point ahead to "our Eucharistic life here in this place"):

> This is the way I understand Jacob's new identity with God. He is blessed, *and* broken. His former life is woven into his future life. He has his same complicated history with his brother, *and* he has a new identity, and a new name. In the course of struggle and in the course of blessing, his private life and his public life, his past and his present are joined together, in a way that has him poised for whatever God has in store for the future. He is blessed *and* he is limping. He has a new name, *and* his whole life story brought him to this moment. Something broken becomes blessed.[13]

---

a love in me for scholarly research and writing. Twenty years later, I published the piece mentioned earlier on matters theological and sexual-political in *Moby-Dick*: "Ishmael's (m)Other."

11. "Donald Trump *Access Hollywood*."
12. Fischer, "Living Inside Out," para. 6.
13. Fischer, "Living Inside Out," para. 7.

Walking Makes the Way

But then Sara moved to Canadian writer Kelly Oxford and her posting this invitation on social media on October 7—the day the *Access Hollywood* tape was released—"Women, tweet me your first [sexual] assaults." Thousands of women responded with the hashtag #notokay. Sara Fischer told us from our ship-prow pulpit she was one of them. Speaking of her assault at the age of twelve, Sara said:

> I didn't fight back. I felt ashamed, and I never told anyone. Later, I totally got over it, I really did. I even forgot about it until five or six years ago when I was doing some writing about women's sexual vulnerability. In that work, the flat strip, the fence between my backstage life and my onstage life became more like a circle, because I was able to connect the story to the rest of my life in a way I hadn't before. Then last week I was having lunch with some friends and we were sharing our stories. All four of us had had similar experiences at twelve or thirteen . . . . In that process [of tweeting Kelly Oxford], mysteriously enough, the circle became the mobius. Something broken became blessed.[14]

A month later, on Sunday, November 13, 2016, five days after the election of Donald Trump to the presidency of the United States, Sara preached what she dubbed her "Bring It On" sermon, a sermon that further illustrated the stance around preaching and politics at St. Paul's. Sara's opening paragraph set the parameters this way:

> This morning's texts [Mal 4:1–2a; 2 Thess 3:6–13, Luke 21:15–19] are perfect for this past week, when many of us have felt betrayed, shocked, anxious, and afraid. And before I say another word I want to acknowledge that not everyone feels this way. It may be that not everyone in this room voted, or not everyone voted for the same person. Voting aside, we are all in a different place on the continuum of trying to imagine what the new administration will mean for us and for many people we love. I also want to acknowledge that personally I resist talking about politics, almost to a fault. But because the election seems to be a license for acts of hate and violence toward vulnerable people, we are beyond politics. We are beyond secular politics, yet we are called to respond. I believe we are called to respond out of our Christian identity.[15]

The body of Sara's sermon named Christianity a "resistance movement." "The Roman government under which first-century Jews lived was

14. Fischer, "Living Inside Out," para. 8.
15. Fischer, "Bring It On," para. 1.

racist, misogynist, xenophobic, corrupt, and economically oppressive. No one in the early church *expected* the government to line up with the love and justice Jesus preached. To be a follower of Jesus was a life-threatening proposition. Today we rarely have to take a stand for the gospel in a way that puts us at risk. [But], as some of you may have imagined over the past few days, this could change."[16]

To join the Christian resistance movement, Sara proclaimed, "is to protect victims of hatred with love. This protection has nothing to do with politics, nothing to do with how we voted or even whether we voted, but with what it means to be a follower of Jesus. Protection may come in the form of advocacy, inclusion, friendship, sanctuary, financial support—and much more."[17]

Sara invited us into specific practices such as praying the Daily Office (morning and evening prayer)—"immers[ing] ourselves in our sweeping scriptural tradition of resistance"; Eucharist—"the realization of a new force at work within the world," in our Sunday worship, as bread and wine are taken, blessed, broken and poured out, and shared equally among all without distinction or preference; not "just coming alongside the vulnerable, but . . . standing between them and those who would do them harm."[18] By "staying close to our baptismal promises" to proclaim by word and example the good news of God in Christ, to seek and serve Christ in all persons, loving our neighbor as ourself, and to strive for justice and peace among all people, respecting the dignity of every human being, which all along have been training us for a social, political, and economic moment such as this, Sara concluded: "As people of the Way, people of hope and promise, I say: Bring it on. Let's be hated because of Jesus' name. Let's be hated because we are truth-tellers and lovers in the name of Christ. Let's astound the world with our love."[19]

So, it was in that space encompassing preaching and politics that I sought a corner in which to provide some shading on the Third Sunday after the Epiphany, January 22, 2017, two days after the inauguration of Donald Trump, the day after the worldwide women's march with all those pink pussy hats. I spent hours and hours watching both events on television, even though that meant holding back much longer than usual on

---

16. Fischer, "Bring It On," paras. 2–3.
17. Fischer, "Bring It On," para. 5.
18. Fischer, "Bring It On," para. 9.
19. Fischer, "Bring It On," paras. 10–11.

finalizing the central moves of my Sunday morning sermon. In particular, I was struck by the difference between the brief time Trump spent out of his car and Barack Obama's long inaugural walk eight years earlier. And images of a lone, white, male, presidential walker juxtaposed to those diverse crowds of marchers around the world—including my daughter and grandsons in Washington, DC, where they live.

If national politics did not pose enough fraught issues for this occasional preacher on January 22, 2017, two significant happenings within the life of the parish also needed to be acknowledged somehow within my sermon. Mother Sara Fischer, our rector, had been away leading a pilgrimage to Israel/Palestine earlier in the month. She had stumbled over a stone bollard in Nazareth and, after several days of painful walking where Jesus walked in days of long ago, relented to having emergency hip replacement surgery in Jerusalem. By January 22, she was back in the United States but in Portland, Oregon, recuperating.

And that Sunday morning marked the inauguration of a long-planned and carefully engineered strategic initiative of Mother Sara's—a dedicated community hour between the 9:00 and 11:15 a.m. masses, in this case, a full, sit down brunch with community-building program. Although we church folk who read the missional literature and were part of those workshops know that community is the correct answer to all questions related to church today, how do we preach community concretely, compellingly, in our cultural context of American hyper-individualism?

We the clergy, vestry, and liturgy planning folk at St. Paul's had agreed weeks earlier that the morning preacher on January 22 (me!) would be scrupulous in delivering a ten-minute homily (not a second more!) to clear sufficient space for the community hour.

Let's get this straight. A briefer than usual sermon composed late Saturday evening, somehow weaving together Trump's inauguration, the women's march, Mother Sara's absence, and the new community hour.

Oh, and in the Revised Common Lectionary Year A cycle of readings, the Third Sunday after the Epiphany is the first time we're invited to consider Matthew's account of the adult, public ministry of Jesus. After the genealogy. After the angel and their announcements. The birth. The holy family. King Herod and the holy innocents. John the Baptist. The baptism of Jesus.

Whew! Here's where I ended up.

So Fill Our Imaginations

"Walking Makes the Way"
The Third Sunday after the Epiphany
Isaiah 9:1–4; Psalm 27:1, 5–13; 1 Corinthians 1:10–18; Matthew 4:12–23
January 22, 2017

> "[Jesus] walked."
>
> —MATTHEW 4:18

Inaugurations are on my mind. Friday's presidential inauguration in Washington, DC, of course. Closer to home—here at St. Paul's, Seattle—we launch one of Mother Sara Fischer's initiatives this morning: a community hour between the 9 o'clock and 11:15 masses. And in our Gospel reading, we hear Matthew's account of the beginning of Jesus' public activity. Inaugurations.

In Matthew's story, Jesus has already been baptized by John in the Jordan River and faced temptation in the Judean wilderness. Then comes an ominous turning point. John is arrested. When Jesus hears the news, he withdraws from Judea, where John was active, and goes back to Galilee. With one crucial difference. Jesus leaves behind the relative safety and security of Nazareth, a secluded village up in the hills, and now makes his home in Capernaum, a busy, commercial city down on the seashore. This geography matters to Matthew and his account of the "Inauguration of Jesus." Matthew knows that Capernaum and neighboring cities lie within the ancient tribal lands of Zebulun and Naphtali. Matthew recalls the prophet Isaiah's promise that God would shine light upon this region, "the way of the sea, the land beyond the Jordan, Galilee of the nations," and restore its joy, despite, no, *because* it was the first Hebrew territory to fall into the gloom of occupation by the Assyrian Empire (Matt 4:13–16; see Isa 9:1–4). Jesus was strategic in choosing Capernaum as home base for his public activity. It straddles the great thoroughfare between Damascus and Egypt. Jesus of *Capernaum*, perhaps, rather than Jesus of *Nazareth*?

☙ ❧

"From that time Jesus *began* to proclaim, 'Repent, for the kingdom of heaven has come near.' As he walked by the Sea of Galilee . . ." (Matt 4:17–18). Remarkable. Jesus' public activity is inaugurated neither with a speech nor a parade. Jesus will have much to say later, and he will be part of a parade

Walking Makes the Way

in Jerusalem near the end of the story—on what we call Palm Sunday. But that is not how it all begins. Nor does the inauguration of Jesus involve a protest march—although Jesus has certainly inspired marchers across the centuries, including some of the millions of women (and men) who marched yesterday in cities all around the world. Instead, Jesus begins his work by going for a walk. A long walk—no little stroll of a hundred yards. A strategic walk throughout all of Galilee. On his walk, according to Matthew, Jesus teaches in synagogues, proclaims the good news of God's kingdom, and cures every disease and sickness among the people. But, I wonder, what if at the inauguration of Jesus, the medium was truly the message? What if walking doesn't just get Jesus to some other place where he teaches and proclaims and heals? Try this: Jesus teaches by walking the way of the sea. Jesus proclaims good news simply for having walked through the busy, occupied cities of Galilee of the nations. In the land beyond the Jordan, far removed from John's baptizing activity, Jesus' walking itself heals.

For there is an even more remarkable feature of Matthew's account of the inauguration of Jesus. From the outset of his long walk, at its very beginning, Jesus chooses not to walk alone. He was all alone in the wilderness when tempted by the devil. But Jesus refuses to walk through the cities of Galilee by himself. He first gathers a community of walking companions around him. Simon Peter and Andrew, then James and John. Follow me. Walk with me. Like Jesus himself leaving Nazareth for Capernaum, the four walking companions leave nets and boat and father behind. And so, the inauguration of Jesus is just as much about inaugurating the community that walks with him. Only in community will Jesus walk the disease and sickness, the bad news, the untruth of those cities. Which is to say, we ourselves receive Jesus' teaching and proclamation and healing only as community.

Later in Matthew's Gospel, Jesus will say: "Where two or three are gathered in my name, I am there among them" (Matt 18:20). Or, for today, how about: where two or three, maybe four or more, walk together following Jesus, he is present among them. Not *in* each one of them as self-contained and complete individuals but among them, *between* them, in all their complementary and contrary differences. Yes, I do believe that as children of one God, we are individually beloved and each called to know this truth and live it from our individual heart of hearts. But when we consider Jesus' public activity, Jesus' long walk, another spiritual law is in force: not without the other, not me without you or you without me, for Jesus is there between us as we walk with him in community. Inaugurating a St. Paul's community hour on Sunday mornings will not make this *true*, but, as with the sacraments, it can make Jesus' presence *real*—tangible and accessible. It may look like we gather in the parish hall around tables and sit in our chairs eating brunch, but really we are companions walking with Jesus.

We have learned from Mother Sara's pilgrimage to Nazareth and Capernaum and Jerusalem, however, that walking is not without risk. We sometimes stumble. Some of us fall. Bones get broken. Lives and institutions falter and get broken. Some of us cannot walk the way at all, or only for a few halting steps with something to hold on to. This makes it all the more essential that Jesus is there between us as community—two or three, if not four or more. Present between those of us with new time and renewed energy for service and those too harried or burned out to take on one more task, however worthwhile. Jesus there between those who can move forward in resistance and those who must retreat out of disappointment or fear. Between the safety and security of a secluded hilltop and the busy-ness and risk down by the seashore—not *in* one of these places, to the exclusion of the other, but *between* them is Jesus present. Between Washington, DC, and Seattle, Washington; between Chicago and Houston, between many generous, talented people in this parish and Mother Sara, absent and recuperating; between those around St. Paul's who have died recently and those who remember and celebrate their lives. There Jesus walks in community, and there God's kingdom comes near in our walking.

ω ∾

A few lines from a poem by Antonio Machado speak to the inaugurations surrounding us this Sunday morning.

> Wayfarer, your footsteps are the way and nothing more.
> Wayfarer, there is no way; the way is made by walking.
> Walking makes the way.[20]

---

20. Machado, "*Caminante no hay camino.*" I discovered this old poem (1907!) through Roberto Goizueta's wonderful book, *Caminemos con Jesús*, 1. I paraphrase in English the lines above from a stanza of Machado's original: "*Caminante, son tus huellas / el camino y nada más; / Caminante, no hay camino, / se hace camino al andar. / Al andar se hace el camino, / y al volver la vista atrás / se ve la senda que nunca / se ha de volver a pisar. / Caminante no hay camino / sino estelas en la mar.*"

Walking Makes the Way

I suspect that for some of you readers, the engagement of politics in my preaching across this year of life in neighborhood, city, country, and world will prove to be far too little; for others, too much. Not just in the foregoing sermon, "Walking Makes the Way," but throughout this book. If so, then I only hope reading my sermons and reflecting upon them clarifies and confirms your own approach and that of your worshipping community, however different from mine.

3

Beyond the Fences

The Conversion of St. Paul the Apostle

PREPARING THIS SERMON REQUIRED a heavy lift from me as occasional preacher. Usually, I know one to three months in advance when I'll be preaching at St. Paul's and on what set of Scripture readings. Not this time. Because of Mother Sara's continued absence as she recuperated from her hip replacement, Deacon Stephen and I swapped preaching duties for Sunday evening, February 17 (when I was originally scheduled to facilitate the shared homily), and Sunday morning, January 29. Which meant me preaching on short notice—no time for my usual luxuriating. Procrastinating? Dawdling? Which disrupted the beautiful pattern of preaching once a month across this particular church year. Which meant preaching two Sunday mornings in a row. With a full week of school in between. Yikes! Which made me appreciate the truly good work of regular preachers like Mother Sara and Father Rob all the more. Their capacity to step up into that pulpit so frequently, week after week.

Because we are a parish who claims Blessed Paul as our patron, St. Paul's is canonically permitted to transfer the Feast of the Conversion of St. Paul the Apostle from January 25 to the Sunday preceding or following and forego celebrating the Third or Fourth Sunday after the Epiphany (depending on the day of the week on which January 6 fell). So, I was responsible for preaching—on short(er) notice (than usual)—at the parish's annual patronal festival. You'll see that I engaged all three of the morning's Scripture readings: first and second and Gospel. This is neither my typical approach nor what the parish expects. And of the three, atypically and maybe unexpectedly, I gave the Gospel reading from Matthew far less attention than the readings from Acts and Galatians. For it poses a challenge on both patronal and lesser feast days, when the story behind a liturgical occasion, such as Paul's conversion, is not carried by the Gospel reading. The appointed Gospel then often seems more generic, as in this case with Matthew 10:16–22.

I'm a theology professor who preaches occasionally. I can do the granular exegetical work with the texts. I love that work. Or is it play? So much so, that I am tempted to dawdle and nerd out and get lost with all those books spread out in front of me on the table, with the Greek interlinear fired up on my tablet. Again, it amazes me how readily regular preachers like Sara or Rob can discern what *this* congregation needs to hear on *this* Sunday from *these* Scripture readings. But maybe that's just their calling, which differs from mine. A conversation with Edward Donalson, my colleague at school, about the multiple pastoral emergencies swirling around him and his sermon and his black Pentecostal worshipping community on a recent Sunday morning drove home the fact that my occasional preaching is inherently less connected to the details of the life situations of the people at St. Paul's, because I don't share the same access as our regular preachers—nor should I. In addition to preaching on Sunday morning or evening, they listen to people's confessions, do pastoral care and baptismal preparation and premarital counseling, anoint people in hospital rooms before surgery, and, in general, hear stories unavailable to me. What I can say about my preaching process is that I require an hour or so, early on, for some completely open-ended musing, savoring, wondering about the readings, before trying to move to my message. In part, that's because images in the lectionary texts tend to draw me in first and tap into whatever spiritual and intellectual energies I possess. In the sermon that follows, for instance, it was the string of verbs and nouns around seeing and sight in the story of Paul's conversion from Acts 26 that provided the homiletical hinge between my launch and the body of my remarks.

Superb pastoral leaders and preachers in a variety of ecclesial contexts have blessed my life's journey. The Revs. Ted Martin, Milton Poole, Timothy Smith, and John Calhoun, in the Church of the Nazarene of my childhood, youth, and early adulthood. The Revs. Joe Williamson, rosie olmstead, Alice Hageman, and Mick Comstock of that urban, progressive, artistic, gay- and lesbian-friendly United Church of Christ congregation in the 1980s. During my brief sojourn with the United Methodists, the Revs. Toby Gould and

Dave Gillespie. And as an Episcopalian, a St. Paul's (Seattle) Episcopalian, for two decades, Fathers and Mothers Morrie Hauge, Wray Mackay, Chuck Ridge, Melissa Skelton, Samuel Torvend, Catharine Reid, and Sara Fischer. They all have richly nourished my faith and practice.

    Which made the advice one of these superb preachers gave to folk learning to preach (or learning to preach better) all the more memorable. I heard Mother Melissa Skelton, when she was rector at St. Paul's and teaching the homiletics class at another theology school in town and taking her class on the road with a series of workshops, warn student preachers to avoid seeking input from others too soon in the process of composing a sermon. For me, it's just the opposite. My preaching is way better when I am situated to hear other voices about texts and contexts as early as possible. I wonder if there's a gendered component to our differing approaches. I wonder if, as a female priest of a particular generation in the Episcopal Church, Melissa had to shut out intentionally the voices of well-meaning male colleagues for fear of not finding her own authentic voice. For me as a cis-gendered man in this social/political/economic and religious culture, I am all too adept at locating and claiming a secure platform on which to stand and from which to speak. My struggle lies in finding a path from detachment and intellect to engagement: heart and hands and feet. Listening to others helps. Listening to women student colleagues at those Tuesday lunchtime brown bag lectionary studies at school often helped grant me permission to access my own experience. As was the case with this sermon on the occasion of Paul's conversion.

"Beyond the Fences"
The Conversion of St. Paul the Apostle (Transferred)
Acts 26:9–21; Psalm 67; Galatians 1:11–24; Matthew 10:16–22
January 29, 2017

"I did not receive [the gospel] from a human source, nor was I taught it."
—GALATIANS 1:12

What does it mean to have a patron saint? What does it mean to have a particular saint—Paul, say, or Andrew—as patron? What does it mean to have a patron saint in a particular place at this particular time? I put those three questions out on Facebook a few days ago. Here's what my friends had to say.

A patron saint is someone whose lifework and wisdom speaks to us today; an advocate who adds his/her voice to the conversation with God on our behalf; someone who nudges a community along through the example of her or his life and is nudged back, as the community reinterprets their patron in light of the present day. Patron saints supply communal or personal identity and vocation. St. Luke the physician inspires the work of health, healing, and wholeness of body at a parish in Renton. St. Veronica calls forth compassion and courage, devotion to accompaniment, from a hospice social worker and member of a religious community. Their wandering Celtic patron who put down the roots of the monastery at Iona shapes the way St. Columba's Church in Kent welcomes people and strives to show up in their local community, shapes even the physical space in which they worship. Right now, at the end of January 2017, the name Thomas More represents longing and belonging, love and comfort and spiritual friendship, while Dominic means safety and solidarity, mutual challenge, gospel-inspired resistance.

What about Paul *our* patron? Some replies from Facebook friends within and beyond this parish. There is no longer Jew or gentile, slave or free, male or female—all of you are one in Christ. The zealous all-in spirit of a missionary coupled with the pragmatism of a tentmaker. A blazing heart on fire for the truth. Clarity of vision and purpose promoting the Christ-message in a postmodern world. Unity and reconciliation in our time of deep division and anxiety. With Paul—and these are my thoughts now—we face an embarrassment of riches. So many of his words and so many stories about him fill Christian Scripture. This leads me to try and trace one single thread through the readings for our patronal Feast of the Conversion of St. Paul the Apostle.

From the Acts of the Apostles (26:9–21), we hear the third of three accounts of the conversion of Paul—or "Paul's Discovery," as it is called in the Godly Play curriculum in whch the children of this parish engage.[1] Paul's *discovery*: how fitting, given the language of sight throughout the story. I *saw* a light from heaven, Paul tells King Agrippa. Get up, Jesus says to Paul,

---

1. Berryman, *Complete Guide*, 4:126–35.

So Fill Our Imaginations

I have *appeared* to you for this purpose; you will testify to the things in which you have *seen* me and in which I will *appear* to you; I send you to the Gentiles to *open their eyes*. And Paul, to the king again, I have not been disobedient to the heavenly *vision*.

All this vision talk means that Paul's discovery is more about Paul being discovered than something Paul discovers. For Paul doesn't find Jesus; Jesus finds him. Paul is on the road to Damascus at midday, when anything and everything he could see on his own was already fully illuminated. Only because the light of Jesus shines brighter than the sun is there something more for Paul to see, something new. How could Paul find Jesus, convinced as he was that he ought to do many things against him: imprisoning the saints of Jerusalem, casting his vote against them when they were being condemned to death, punishing them in all the synagogues to try to force them to blaspheme; furiously enraged at the followers of Jesus, pursuing them even to foreign cities? No, Paul was seeking in order to destroy the name of Jesus of Nazareth. But Jesus found Paul and transformed Paul the persecutor of the followers of Jesus into a follower himself. The Godly Play lesson puts it this way: "Paul was to travel to the ends of the earth and tell people what had happened to him, for he had changed. His work was to try to say how his hate had turned to love and to begin churches where people could show how this was done. He was also to write letters to help new churches do this."[2]

This morning's reading from the letter to the Galatians suggests that Paul *caught* the good news of hate changed to love; he was not *taught* it. Paul admits he had been taught much in his earlier life. He advanced beyond many among his people and was far more zealous for their traditional ways. But the gospel Paul comes to proclaim, he says, "is not of human origin; for I did not receive it from a human source, nor was I taught it, but I received it through a revelation of Jesus Christ" (Gal 1:11–12). *Caught* beyond what he had been *taught*. And after receiving this revelation, Paul continues, "I did not confer with any human being, nor did I go up to Jerusalem to those who were already apostles before me" (Gal 1:16–17). Paul takes his revelation, his being discovered by Jesus, to the Arabian desert for three years. Years of prayer, of watching the empty desert and listening to its silence. Then Paul—outsider to the established leadership of the churches of Jesus Christ—claims authority to go to other places those other apostles could not or would not go, to the gentiles, to fellow outsiders.

---

2. Berryman, *Complete Guide*, 4:133.

Beyond the Fences

Paul's discovery. Finding by being found. Caught, not taught. Jesus calls to just such a discovery, and promises it, in this morning's Gospel reading from Matthew. Be *wise* and *innocent*: "Do not worry about how you are to speak or what you are to say; for what you are to say will be given to you at the time; for it is not you who speak, but the Spirit of [God] speaking through you" (Matt 10:19–20).

⁂

Now for the sake of my professorial reputation, I want you to know that in addition to posting my questions about patron saints on Facebook, I was part of a little lectionary study this past week. A woman in the group—not connected to St. Paul's, not an Episcopalian, preparing to preach on the Beatitudes at her United Church of Christ congregation this morning—said the readings from Acts and Galatians and Matthew reminded her of Carl Jung's favorite story, the story of the water and the well.[3]

The water of life, wishing to make itself available on the surface of the earth, bubbled up in an artesian well and flowed without effort or limit. People came to drink of the water and were nourished by it, since it was so clean and invigorating. But gradually, a few worried that they needed to protect the water of life, to preserve its purity and keep it from running out. So, they began to build fences around the well and charge fees for drinking the water. They claimed ownership of the property around the well, passing laws as to who could approach it. They put locks on the gates. Still, the people came.

The water of life became angry. It retreated back underground and began to bubble up in another place beyond the fences. Water still flowed in the original well, but it was no longer the water of life. The owners of the property were so engrossed in their schemes they did not notice the change. They started bottling and selling the non-life-giving water. And still the people came—or most of them. A few went beyond the fences and were found by the water of life as it bubbled up in a new well. Eventually, however, fences were built again to control access to the water, and the whole cycle repeated itself over and over—each time with the water flowing somewhere else, where it could find and be found and give life once more.

That's Jung's story of the water and the well.

---

3. Thanks to Karyn Frazier for the helpful discussion on Tuesday and to Lowell Chilton, too. The story of the water and the well is mentioned by Robert A. Johnson in his book *Owning Your Own Shadow*, vii–viii.

So Fill Our Imaginations

Before his discovery, Paul was skilled at maintaining fences of hatred and control. On his way to extend such a fence, Paul strayed beyond and stayed beyond. As our patron, Paul invites us out beyond the fences. To be found by love and find our hatred changed to love. To catch what we need to teach. Among outsiders.

You find in "Beyond the Fences" my first explicit mention of Godly Play, the Montessori-based program of children's religious formation used at St. Paul's and other congregations within and beyond the Episcopal Church. There will be several more such mentions in this book. A few initial words on the subject here.

It was 2007, days before my fifty-fourth birthday, and my first grandchild—a boy—came into the world. My other daughter then had boys in 2009 and 2012. But my two girls and their three boys live in Minnesota and Maryland. I loved being a grandparent immediately but missed not being able to spend more time with the grandsons. With children! So, partially as compensation, partially as calling to a new ministry, I decided to get trained to teach Godly Play. Students in their thirties, forties, fifties, and sixties, Monday through Friday at school, then three- to five-year-olds or first- to third-graders at church on Sunday mornings! This experience of being around children in a faith context has been as formative for me as anything else these past dozen years. Children have encouraged me to be more playful in relation to liturgy, to Scripture—dare I say to self and God? Children's responses and reflections have called me back to the trunk of the gospel tree from all those luxuriant leaves and fruit way out on the end of the church's branches. And that's good news, I believe, for the adults in my classrooms at school and in front of me in the pews or beside me on the chairs when I preach on Sundays.

In addition to being a Montessori educator, the creator of the Godly Play curriculum, Jerome Berryman, is an Episcopal priest. And so it should not be surprising that the ideal Godly Play lesson mirrors the classic *ordo* or shape of Christian eucharistic worship: gathering, word, meal, sending. Children and an adult storyteller *gather*, sit together, and form and hold a circle on the floor of the classroom. A second adult serves as doorkeeper, safeguarding the threshold between Godly Play space, time, and dynamics and those that operate outside the room. Once ready, the children hear a lesson presented by the storyteller, engage the story verbally as a group, often through wondering questions, then respond to the *word* creatively, each in a manner of their own choosing. Next, paralleling the eucharistic *meal*, adults and children share a "feast" of simple food and drink with conversation around the circle, first praying over the fruit, crackers, cheese sticks, and water (or whatever). Finally, the storyteller offers each child a warm blessing and they are *sent* out to parents, parish community, and wider world by the doorkeeper.[4]

Godly Play encourages me, as an Anglican Christian, to hold together the drama of embodied Catholic sacramental action and the disciplined Protestant attunement to Scripture. As a (post)modern, Godly Play puts me more deeply in touch with elemental forms of human experience, such as oral storytelling. As an adult, Godly Play recasts my Christian faith, clearing out some of the clutter, making it more tangible and more nimble, altogether more wonderful and wonder-filled. But further thoughts about the spiritual and theological impact of Godly Play on my preaching will have to wait for more appropriate junctures. In the meantime, let me wrap up commentary on the foregoing third sermon.

I have a diminutive presence on social media. My mother, in her seventies at the time, had a Facebook page before I did; my then twenty-, thirty-something daughters, likewise. Most of the time (and that means monthly, maybe, not daily or hourly), I just post photos to Facebook. Often of nature—ashfall on my car from wildfires in the mountains, an Oregon junco drinking from a dripping hose on the back deck. I enjoy creating captions to go with my photos: "Nosy dahlias . . . ," to accompany a picture of several blossoms peeking in the dining room window, to which a Facebook friend and coreligionist at St. Paul's replied in kind: "Off with their heads!" On the occasion of this sermon, however, social media managed to convene additional, insightful voices around my task of preaching on short notice about patron saints, St. Paul, and his conversion.

I know some preachers routinely reach out via social media of all sorts ahead of their sermons with ideas and questions and confessions of being totally stymied. Maybe I should, too, for a disproportionate number of my two hundred Facebook friends are active church folk, leaders even, and academic types—former students, colleagues from a number of schools, pastors and lay leaders across the ecclesial spectrum. But I don't. Across

---

4. See Berryman, *Complete Guide*, 1:51–74.

So Fill Our Imaginations

the entire year of preaching, this was the only time friends on social media showed up in a sermon of mine.

4

Coming by Night, Being Born to Daylight
[Remarks for Shared Homily]
The Second Sunday in Lent

OF THE TWELVE SERMONS gathered together here, this was the first one delivered at a 5:00 p.m. Sunday mass, what we around St. Paul's describe as a shared homily. Recall what I said in the introduction to this book about preaching at the parish's evening service. The preacher's primary task is to facilitate the community's response to the scriptural texts, liturgical occasion, and experiential context, rather than preclude it or make it redundant. The goal is open-ended remarks inviting verbal engagement throughout the room by any and all.

Sometimes, during some seasons of the church year, the work of artists-in-residence offers the 5:00 p.m. community an additional way in to worship, generally, and the shared task of proclaiming the word, specifically. Photographers, painters, several poets and actors and musicians, a dancer, and an installation artist have all served in this capacity. It's the liturgy planning team for the 5:00 p.m. Sunday mass who, in consultation with the rector, selects and invites the artists. And for better or for worse, the members of the planning team reflect the social location(s) of parish members as a whole: predominantly white, more women than men, a significant minority LGBTQ+ (30 or 40 percent?). When an artist-in-residence is present, the second reading from the lectionary, the epistle reading, is omitted, and engagement with the artist's work happens at that point in the service. When the art is visual or tactile, the gathered worshippers stand up and move around the room to stations where the art is displayed. When it is a musician, poet, or actor, the assembly stays put, although the artist may move around. The work of the artist adds one more "word" to the evening. Not the last word, for the proclamation of the Gospel and shared homily always follow.

The 5:00 p.m. liturgy planning team gives special attention to the seasons of Advent, Lent, and Easter. That's typically when we engage artists-in-residence. Sometimes the planning team even proposes seasonal and/or weekly themes. During Eastertide 2014 (also Year A!), for example, under the broad rubric "Meeting Jesus in New Ways," the following specific weekly themes emerged, suggested by the Gospel readings: meeting Jesus in the wounded (John 20), at a table that transforms the journey (Luke 24), as a threshold (John 10), where we live (John 14), in "other" places (John 14), and as he disappears (John 17). These weekly themes were offered as guidance to the preachers as well as to the artist-in-residence. Other seasonal themes have included "Casting Off and Putting On" (Advent 2012), "Nourishment" (Lent 2013), and "Becoming Whole" (Easter 2015).

The 2017 Lenten season was a little different. A poet, Anne Doe-Overstreet, did indeed serve as artist-in-residence. But not for the 5:00 p.m. community alone. Worshippers at the morning masses could hear Anne read one of her poems each week at that new community hour between the 9:00 and 11:15 services. The same poem she would then offer in the evening as part of the worship service. Fragments from each poem were excerpted, beautifully calligraphed by Deacon Stephen Crippen on large sheets of fabric, and hung on rough sticks as banners in the parish hall—site of both the morning community hour and the evening mass. No overarching seasonal theme was chosen for 2017, however, other than the Lenten, catechetical, coming-to-faith, preparation-for-baptism ones embedded in the classic Gospel readings retained in Year A of the Revised Common Lectionary (from Jesus' temptation to the raising of Lazarus, by way of Nicodemus, the Samaritan woman at the well, and the man born blind). So, on the evening of March 12, 2017, we did not hear the appointed epistle reading (Rom 4:1–5, 13–17) but listened to the (unpublished) poem "Under Cover of Dark" by Anne Doe-Overstreet instead—reproduced here with Anne's permission. The subject of the poem is Nicodemus.

Coming by Night, Being Born to Daylight

What he notices, the sweetened sky
inked in outside the open door,
the palm-washed atmosphere.
He's arrived to find the strange

served up in metaphor of water-troubled
wind that winds, rootless, past the self.
The images escape his grasp: age-diminished
flesh and desert snakes on sticks.

What if, in that, the smallest hour—
balanced scale of day and dark—
what if a life and yet
again, a life occurs to him,

unbridled, wildly cosmic?
With the suddenness of flight,
how stumbled must his going back
have been, before his pacing found its stride

beneath the cover of the night inspired
by some half-formed thought that gyroscoped
around that room. Alleyways and city roads now
around him stretch away; the prospect overhead

expands to compass in the long-lit dead of suns,
life-given twice—the once to born and burn
as stars, the next to light the birth
that gilds and graces even gold-blind sight.

    I have frequently facilitated the shared homily when the work of an artist-in-residence has been alive in the evening worship experience. At first, it made me really anxious as preacher to have this other element *in* the mix but *out* of my control. Eventually, I relaxed into the artist-in-residence's work as one more improvisational aspect of our 5:00 p.m. Sunday mass. I gave up any compulsive need to know ahead of time what the poem or musical piece or photograph was going to be. I think I've learned to listen to or view the work of the artist-in-residence well enough to incorporate an open-ended question about it on the fly, so people could comment during the shared homily, if they chose to do so.

    I reiterate what I said earlier. With the following reduced-to-writing-and-printed-sermon, you will be reading only my remarks aimed to invite

So Fill Our Imaginations

and incite one particular gathering of 5:00 p.m. worshippers' reflections and words. You will not, cannot, read the entire shared homily from March 12, 2017, because those other voices are absent here. Preaching in the evening feels more oral to me, more conversational, than at the morning masses. The written text provides at best a reconstruction of what I, alone, spoke.

Nevertheless . . .

"Coming by Night, Being Born to Daylight"
[Remarks for Shared Homily]
The Second Sunday in Lent
Genesis 12:1–4a; Psalm 121; John 3:1–17
March 12, 2017

"So it is with everyone who is born of the Spirit," Jesus says (John 3:8). *How* is it, we might ask, with those born of the Spirit? And how might it be *with us*?

Nicodemus the Pharisee comes to Jesus by night, under cover of darkness, to protect his reputation as a leader of the people. He comes with an inkling of Jesus' significance, although his awkward questions betray a lack of deeper insight. Something draws Nicodemus. He comes by night, yes; but he does come to Jesus, against all odds. Where to begin? What to say? "Rabbi, we know that you are a teacher who has come from God; for no one can do these signs that you do apart from the presence of God" (John 3:2). Nicodemus's first words sound so full of certainty: Jesus, *we know who you are*. But maybe Nicodemus lacks language to express what he longs for most deeply. Maybe his seemingly certain declaration, we *know*, is just a safe, noncommittal way to get a conversation going. Maybe it serves as a defense mechanism, covering up uncertainty. Maybe his statement disguises a question: *who are you*? Maybe the bold, plural *we* know, wraps a security blanket around a lonely, vulnerable *I* don't know.

Jesus' first response to Nicodemus, "Very truly, I tell you, no one can see the kingdom of God without being born from above [or, born anew]" (3:3), makes sense only if Jesus can discern the true longing hidden behind false certainty and self-protection. Only if Jesus hears the whispering of Nicodemus's heart: I want to live and act and relate the way you do; I want to join the community around you; I long for a new and freer and more spacious life.

Coming by Night, Being Born to Daylight

There's a reason Nicodemus comes to Jesus by night, the same reason we might. The night protects us. Under cover of darkness, we feel free to bring our whole selves—our uncertainty, our struggles, and our deepest longing. Jesus accepts exactly *what* we and Nicodemus bring and *who* we bring. No need to dress our self up or sanitize it or sugarcoat it. There is grace in coming by night. With the privacy night affords, we find courage to say something we were afraid to say in daylight.

So it is with everyone who is born of the Spirit.

How can anyone be born after having grown old, Nicodemus goes on to ask? Can one enter a second time into the mother's womb and be born? As if to object: as an elder in the religious community constrained by tradition, my identity and world view are certain and fixed—no transformation possible here. Jesus answers: "Very truly, I tell you, no one can enter the kingdom of God without being born of water and Spirit. What is born of the flesh is flesh, and what is born of the Spirit is spirit.... The wind blows where it chooses and you hear the sound of it, but you do not know where it comes from or where it goes" (vv. 5–6, 8). This second response makes sense only if the wind of the Spirit is already blowing through Nicodemus. He hears its sound—without knowing the origin of his longing or its destination. The wind will roar, and Nicodemus will be blown away. Born anew. Born from above. For this is just the first time we hear of Nicodemus in the Gospel of John. Later, he pushes back against his fellow religious leaders in the semiprivacy of a council meeting when they make plans to destroy Jesus (John 7:45–52). Does our law permit someone to be condemned without due process, he asks? And at the end of John's Gospel, Nicodemus brings a hundred pounds of myrrh and aloes to help Joseph of Arimathea bury the body of the crucified Jesus—now publicly and in broad daylight (John 19:38–42).

With the Spirit, there is the possibility of shedding our old skin and self, the possibility of rebirth, of our new self. Our artist-in-residence, Anne Doe-Overstreet, evoked and invoked such transformation in her poem: "a life and yet again, a life," she writes; "life-given twice—the once to born and burn / as stars, the next to light the birth / that gilds and graces even gold-blind sight." There is grace in coming by night and there is also the next grace of being born to daylight. Jesus detects birth pains in Nicodemus and in us. He welcomes our disguised and awkward questions, teasing from them hints of deeper insight. He draws us out into productive uncertainty, instead of shutting us down and closing us in with premature answers. But,

So Fill Our Imaginations

as was true for Nicodemus, Jesus refuses to let us off the hook. In due time, he also refuses to ignore the fact that we have work to do, that we need new birth and growth and healing—that these represent our deepest longing.

So it is with everyone who is born of the Spirit.

I wonder how and when you have experienced the grace of coming by night and the next grace of being born to daylight? I wonder how and when you have offered one or the other of these two graces to someone else? And I wonder, as this Sunday afternoon turns to evening and moves on toward night, if you hear the spontaneous, mysterious sound of the Spirit of transformation? I invite your response: to my words, to the work of our artist-in-residence, to any of our Scriptures, or to this occasion, the Second Sunday in Lent.

Some years into the life of Sunday Evenings at St. Paul's, sitting in a monthly liturgy planning team meeting and looking around at the six or seven of us involved, I was stunned by the sudden realization that every single one of us was a trained, experienced Godly Play teacher! This fact explains much about the liturgical-theological-spiritual proclivities of the 5:00 p.m. mass and its distinctive ethos, at least as I experience them.[1]

Grounded in Montessori educational theory and praxis, Jerome Berryman's Godly Play is more like group spiritual direction for children than traditional Sunday School. Godly Play assumes the full humanity of children; assumes children already possess spiritual depth and legitimate theological insights of their own, without being spoon-fed watered-down adult constructs. According to Berryman, Godly Play seeks to provide a safe place for children to discover their own authentic experience of God and, gradually, with adult assistance, "to learn the art of how to identify this experience and express, refine, name, value, and wonder about it in the most appropriate language and action."[2]

---

1. Alissabeth Newton was one of the Godly Play instructors present at that Sunday evening liturgy planning team meeting. In addition to coauthoring the article on the 5:00 p.m. liturgy at St. Paul's mentioned earlier, "Praying at the Edges," we have also published in the area of child theology. See our "Playing with Pictures of Paradox."

2. Berryman, *Children and the Theologians*, 7.

Coming by Night, Being Born to Daylight

I sense two primary gifts Godly Play has offered our 5:00 p.m. worshipping community. For starters, the church-in-the-round physical layout of Sunday evening worship at St. Paul's mirrors the circle of adult storyteller and children in Godly Play. Neither the Godly Play teacher nor the children are at the center of this circle. Instead, the materials that prompt and carry the adult's words are placed in the empty space marked out by the circle, whether three-dimensional figurines or objects, plaques with images printed on them, or simple flat figures cut from felt, cardboard, or laminated paper. Similarly, at the 5:00 p.m. mass, worship happens in a circle around the altar and across from one another. At the center, one finds the table for the eucharistic meal. Literally and figuratively, the pulpit is decentered, as is the ordained clergyperson. We resist cultural and ecclesial impulses to focus on an individual person or a specific thing. The focal point is an empty space, the space between people gathered in community. The altar is the thing that makes the emptiness at the center of the circle apparent and so, in a sense, is no-thing.[3]

With its Godly Play-like circle, Sunday Evenings at St. Paul's enacts the Lukan story of the road to Emmaus (Luke 24:13–35). For the first half of the liturgy, the table is empty. It promises a meal that is to come and suggests that our gathering is not complete until the eucharistic feast. A conversation with and about Scripture occurs but only on our journey to the meal, across the empty altar where Jesus will be fully known only in the breaking of the bread. Once recognized as the Lord, Jesus disappears, and we must rise, go back to the city, the place of trauma and of service, to tell others and find him again.

Second, consider how the practice of a shared homily at St. Paul's 5:00 p.m. Sunday mass aims to incarnate Montessori values of an open classroom, foundational to Godly Play, especially the "wondering questions." It's no accident that the words "I wonder . . ." appear on the front covers of Godly Play curriculum books. That form of inquiry is essential. In many Godly Play lessons, after a highly visual and/or tactile presentation of a biblical story, the life of a saint, or some aspect of Christian life, the adult storyteller will pose a series of "I wonder . . ." questions to the circle of children, prompting their reflection and verbal response. For instance, after retelling Jesus' parable of the leaven, the Godly Play curriculum suggests the storyteller might ask the children: "Now, I wonder if the woman [who hid the leaven in the flour mixture] has a name? I wonder who she could

---

3. To improvise on a theme from Rowan Williams; see his "Between the Cherubim."

really be? I wonder if the woman was happy? I wonder what the leaven is, really, in the parable and in life? I wonder if you could take the bread that was leavened all over and put it back like it was before the woman hid the leaven in it? I wonder if you have ever come close to a place where this happens? I mean, really, not just in parable or making bread?"[4]

Berryman writes about the role of wondering questions:

> The storyteller invites the children to wonder about the lesson.... There are no predetermined answers to a wondering question. As Godly Play teachers our job is to support the process of wondering, not to approve or disapprove of specific answers. The children's wondering emerges out of their own lives, their relationships with God and their participation in the lesson. Let God be there. Allow this powerful language to do its work. Trust the searching of the children to find what they need with God and the Scriptures.[5]

Substitute "preacher" or "person facilitating" for Berryman's words "storyteller" and "teacher," and "members of the congregation" or "those seated around the altar and across from one another" for "children," and you have my take on the why and wherefore of our shared homily. For downstairs on Sunday evening at St. Paul's, all members of the assembly stand and sit on the same level. There is no raised platform for a few. The preacher facilitating the shared homily does so seated, like the rest of the congregation. And to be shared, the preacher's part of the homily must end with questions, not answers. Most often employing precisely the "I wonder..." form championed by Godly Play, as I did above on the Second Sunday in Lent in transitioning from my remarks to the community's reflection and response: "I wonder how and when you have experienced the grace of coming by night and the next grace of being born to daylight? I wonder...? And I wonder...?"

If you spend enough time around Godly Play, you'll begin to hear talk of a "hidden lesson"—those convictions and values, that worldview, conveyed not through the explicit content of a lesson but in how the telling of the story unfolds in space and time, with deep respect for persons and materials, above all by honoring and holding the circle. After worshipping for a decade in the evening at St. Paul's, I find that this particular liturgy offers its own hidden lesson in the form of a creative and peaceful theological resistance/reformation. It resists patriarchy through female priest-presiders,

---

4. Berryman, *Complete Guide*, 3:114.
5. Berryman, *Complete Guide*, 1:56.

queer preachers, artists-in-residence, the around and across of the assembly, a more accessible liturgy for both children and parents. It re-forms hierarchy, again through the physical layout of the worship space, as well as intimacy with the altar/table, and the shared homily. This liturgical and homiletical rendering of church and community, of human being and God in Christ, constitutes a nonviolent but subversive critique of, and alternative to, dominant cultural values of individualism, consumerism, exclusion, and hatred of the body, of women, and of children.[6]

---

6. I have always appreciated how Letty Russell grounds her feminist view of the church upon the image of a circle of people seated around and across. See her *Church in the Round*.

5

Touching Is Believing
[Remarks for Shared Homily]
The Second Sunday of Easter

OCCASIONAL PREACHERS KNOW THE Second Sunday of Easter all too well: "Low" Sunday. Seminarians. Interns and others doing their field work. Theology school faculty. Retired priests in the diocese. Almost anyone, to give the parish clergy, the regular preachers, a breather, after their exertions preparing multiple sermons on multiple occasions for Holy Week and Easter Sunday. I'm no exception. I have preached on this occasion several times. And year in and year out, Lectionary Years A, B, and C, the Gospel is always the Thomas story from John 20. The only other Sunday in the church year on which this occasional preacher has been asked to preach as regularly is Trinity Sunday. Let the house theologian have a go at that one!

As a theology professor, part of my calling is to make things more complex. To encounter, as I say in an introductory class session on "What Is Theology?," the familiar as unfamiliar and the unfamiliar as familiar. Not to complexify things just for the fun (or spite) of it but to dig beneath the surface of *both* the religious tradition(s) we inherit from the ancestors *and* our own individual and communal experience(s) here and now—to cast into higher relief the cultural differences between the wisdom of our religious heritage(s) and the contemporary human situation(s), as well as to discern ways to bridge the gap between tradition and experience. An example I often use involves the intertwined stories of Jesus, Jairus's daughter, and the woman with the hemorrhages in Mark 5. A web of stories that turn on gender; male and female embodiment; power, privilege, and access (or the lack thereof); pollution and purity; life and death. And stories that turn those binaries all inside out.

The core of my work in preparing remarks for this 5:00 p.m. Sunday shared homily involved tracing commonalities and divergences within half a dozen stories from John's Gospel that the lectionary sets forth in Year A for Lent and beyond. (Matthew on hiatus for a time.) The image of Thomas *touching* Jesus in chapter 20 led me to dig deeper into the way the central Johannine theme of *believing* gets enfleshed in those earlier stories, as *seeing* or *hearing* or *being touched by* Jesus.

As was the case with the previous sermon in this series, the shared homily for Sunday evening, March 12 (the Second Sunday in Lent), the 5:00 p.m. community was engaging the work of an artist-in-residence during the 2017 Easter season, this time, an actor, Christine Brown, who portrayed scenes from the life of Dorothy Day. So, once again for the Second Sunday of Easter, Low Sunday, the second reading appointed by the lectionary (1 Pet 1:3–9) was omitted. Christine offered her art in its place. Then the Gospel was proclaimed (the Thomas story), and I moved my chair in front of the lectern to facilitate the community's shared homily with the remarks that follow.

"Touching Is Believing"
[Remarks for Shared Homily]
The Second Sunday of Easter
Acts 2:14a, 22–32; Psalm 16; John 20:19–31
April 23, 2017

Now Jesus did many other signs which are not written in this book. But these *are* written, so that you may believe and have life (John 20:30–31).

Over the past six weeks, we have read one story after another from the Gospel of John. Stories of believing and stories of living. I have repeatedly found myself in these stories. I wonder if you have found yourself in them as well? They are meant to be stories we live into and by which we believe.

Maybe, like Nicodemus, I can come to new life only by night, under cover of darkness (John 3).

So Fill Our Imaginations

Maybe, like the Samaritan woman at the well, you need someone to tell you everything you have ever done (John 4).

Like the man born blind, sometimes we need to have our eyes smeared with mud; or, like Lazarus, we need the help of others to unbind us and let us go; or, like all the disciples in the house, we need our feet washed by Jesus (John 9, 11, 13).

This evening—with Thomas—we have one final story from the Gospel of John. All those earlier stories were about hearing and believing. Seeing. Drinking the water of life. Being freed and being washed. Being touched *by* Jesus. The Thomas story is different. It's about Thomas *touching* Jesus.

Some things, in order to be believed and for us to have life, we need to touch them. Sometimes, touching is believing.

To touch Jesus, Thomas must return to the house where the disciples met—that house so full of memory. For touching to be believing, Thomas must reach out his hand. For Thomas to touch is to put himself physically, viscerally, into the truth of Jesus.

Jesus invites Thomas to touch him. Touching is believing when it is a response to the living, loving one.

Thomas touches Jesus' wounds. Thomas identifies with Jesus' wounded-ness, making it his own.

By touching, by reaching out his hand to wounded-ness, Thomas rejoins the community of fellow believers. Putting himself into Jesus' wounds heals Thomas's estrangement from the others in the house. Touching is believing, and believing is living.

So, I wonder what, in order to be believed, you need to touch and not just see or hear?

I wonder when, for you to have life, is touching believing?

And I wonder what connections there might be between the Thomas story and that of Dorothy Day in the work of our artist-in-residence or any other aspect of our shared experience on this Second Sunday of Easter? I invite your responses.

This was by far the briefest of my twelve sermons. Brief even by Episcopal Church standards, those of St. Paul's (Seattle), and of our Sunday evening mass. Maybe I, too, was exhausted from Holy Week, if not from preaching

Touching Is Believing

then by serving liturgically at six of our eight services beginning at 7:30 a.m. on Palm Sunday and not ending until early afternoon on Easter Sunday. Or maybe what was needful for all of us, myself included, was to sit contemplatively with just a few words. I worked to slow my delivery way down in order to make more palpable the image of touching as believing.

6

To an Unknown God in Whom We Live and Move and Have Our Being

The Sixth Sunday of Easter

I INTRODUCED YOU EARLIER to Sophia, the baby carrying trisomy 18 in every cell of her body. Sophia was stillborn on April 28, 2017. Her requiem mass was held at St. Paul's on Friday, May 5. Mother Sara Fischer preached a sermon entitled "Marvelously Made," alluding to Psalm 139—a biblical text Sara and baby Sophia's parents had discussed together months earlier, while Sophia was alive in her mother's womb. I was there at the funeral, vested and serving in the liturgy. A service held upstairs, even though baby Sophia and her parents regularly attended the 5:00 p.m. Sunday mass downstairs. But they were accustomed to worshipping in that other space on high holy days, such as Ash Wednesday, Maundy Thursday, and the Great Vigil and First Mass of Easter.

I listened to the words of Mother Sara's sermon. Words about our "powerless[ness] to do anything in the face of [such] tragic loss"; about being able to "do nothing but grieve," which "won't be enough."[1] But words also about how, at that very moment back in December when Sara and baby Sophia's parents were eating and talking about Psalm 139, "God was knitting Sophia together in [her mother's] womb, . . . fashioning Sophia's tiny limbs, day by day, limbs that would soon begin kicking like any other

---

1. Fischer, "Marvelously Made," para. 2.

To an Unknown God in Whom We Live and Move and Have Our Being

baby in the womb, saying 'I am here.'"[2] It is God who gets to decide what it means to be marvelously made. "In God's eyes, Sophia was perfect from head to toe from before she was even a twinkle in her parents' eyes all the way through eternity. Marvelously made."[3] For if we learn anything from Psalm 139, Sara went on, "it is that God never leaves us alone; we cannot escape God's knowledge or God's handiwork. It is everywhere."[4]

As I listened, an insight visited me, spiritual and theological, but also profoundly carnal, fleshy. Visceral, even. The only environment baby Sophia had ever known was her mother's womb! Her only world. Only universe. Or, said the other way around, baby Sophia experienced her mother's womb as the entire universe: the whole of reality, infinite and all-encompassing. Which placed Sophia in the words Paul quotes in Acts 17, words the lectionary appointed as part of the readings for my next preaching assignment three Sundays after Sophia's requiem: her mother was the one *in whom baby Sophia lived and moved and had her being*. An image for all of us, all things, living and moving and having their being in God, as mother, as womb.

Oh, I had other thoughts during and after baby Sophia's funeral. How tiny and how beautiful the little box containing her ashes was, as I held it for a time in the Bolster Memorial Garden. Life and death. Death in the midst of life. Birth and second birth. For one stillborn? Born to eternal life. Elijah, taken up from earth into heaven without dying. From the passion of Friday to Sunday's resurrection, with no sabbath rest in a tomb in between, on Holy Saturday?

Many of my thoughts emerged from and immersed themselves back in the deeply baptismal character of the Episcopal Church's service for the burial of the dead. I felt keenly the ever-so-appropriate and yet throat-catching absence of two petitions during the prayers of the people concerning Sophia and baptism and eucharist. "For our sister Sophia," we did indeed pray "to our Lord Jesus Christ who said 'I am Resurrection and I am Life.'" We prayed: "You wept at the grave of Lazarus your friend; comfort us in our sorrow" and "You raised the dead to life; give our sister eternal life." But we omitted: our sister "was washed in Baptism" and "nourished with your Body and Blood."[5] Until the week after the funeral, a female, Roman

---

2. Fischer, "Marvelously Made," para. 4.
3. Fischer, "Marvelously Made," para. 5.
4. Fischer, "Marvelously Made," para. 6.
5. Episcopal Church, *Book of Common Prayer*, 497.

So Fill Our Imaginations

Catholic colleague at school took my breath away by just flat out saying to my face that baby Sophia *had been baptized* in the waters of her mother's womb *and communed* with her blood. My colleague spoke of the baptism of the martyrs. And so, I ended up days later—spiritually and theologically—where baby Sophia's requiem mass had begun physically: in the St. Paul's entryway, or better, its baptistery. And I recalled, now with deeper power and meaning, that while our new baptismal font had originally been sketched out before the building renovation began to have a sharp, rectilinear, sarcophagus-like shape, it ended up round and womb-like, with living water trickling down from an upper bowl or basin into a lower one.

St. Paul's Baptismal Font

My initial thought was: baby Sophia lived and moved and had her being entirely within her mother's womb. This insight called up for me the resources of process theology—a second indispensable item in my theological (and homiletical) toolkit, along with feminist and womanist theology. I summarized earlier the primary conviction I draw from process theology this way: God is most, not least, related to all other beings; all reality exists within the encompassing reality of God; hence, might it not be more appropriate to think of the God-world relationship in terms of metaphors of expressive body and animating spirit, of gestation, rather than artist and their work? A pan-*en*-theistic view of God and the world. All *in* God, by contrast to both traditional pantheism (God *is* all / all *is* God, with no differentiation) and traditional theism (with God and the world as fundamentally *different* beings or modes of reality).

Now some of you know that process theology possesses a rich storehouse of technical conceptualities and jargon, for which panentheism serves merely as a kind of sign on the front gate. I have published academic work that utilizes these terms and concepts.[6] But I have never considered myself a card-carrying member of some process theology club or party. The resources of process theology help me make better sense of God and the world. When I wrestle with other central theological issues (humanity, Jesus the Christ, church, etc.), I am aided instead by other theologies and their approaches. My attraction to process theology, however, has autobiographical roots. As a teenager and young adult in the 1960s and 70s, the question of what it might mean to speak of God's presence in and relationship to the world, *our* world, was posed existentially by the collision between my childhood experience of friendship with Jesus and racial injustice in America, the Vietnam War, the overthrow of Salvador Allende in Chile, and government-aided-and-abetted famines in Nigeria and Ethiopia. Colleague-students in my introductory theology class and I play around seriously with how basic theological questions and convictions grow out of our autobiographies. Accounts by James Cone and Sallie McFague enable our classroom discussion.[7]

Hence, in more popular writing, in workshops and retreats, and, yes, in sermons, I have been more concerned to share the moral, spiritual, and practical gifts of process theology with folk than the metaphysical ones. With a female coauthor, I have juxtaposed a view of God as attentive and nurturing parent to the experience some people have of God as absent or abusive, penning lines such as:

> God's very nature is expressed in what we have called the receptive and active sides of love. To say God *is* love means that God allows all people (as well as all God's creatures) to make a real difference in

---

6. M. L. Taylor, *God Is Love*, especially 335–407; and "Boundless Love of God."

7. Cone, "Looking Back, Going Forward"; and McFague, *Life Abundant*, 3–24. Cone has greatly elaborated the autobiographical matrix of his theology in *Said I Wasn't Gonna Tell Nobody*.

> God's life, and, because of the real difference they make, God acts toward all people so as to assist them to develop fully as persons.[8]

And:

> To say that God's love, like ours, has a receptive side means that we have an effect on God. Does this mean we change God? No and yes. Nothing we are or do can change the fact that God is God. Nothing we are or do can change the fact that God is love. Nothing we are or do can change the fact that God's love is all-powerful, eternal, and all-wise. In other words, God's character, God's personality, God's "Godness" are utterly unchangeable and are not affected by us. What is changed, although this is not quite the right word since we usually think of change being a weakness, is God's actual experience. It is not so much change as it is involvement. God is aware of us as we are. The alternative would be to say that God would remain literally the same whether we were rejoicing or grieving, honest or dishonest, burned-out or healthy. That is the idolatrous image of God as Absent Parent again.[9]

I have appealed to Psalm 103 and to the parable of the prodigal father (= prodigal son) in Luke 15 as biblical portraits of a panentheistic view of God, without ever using that big word.[10] In the sermon that follows, it's in relation to the phrase from Acts 17, "in whom we live and move and have our being," that I hoped my hearers might reflect a little on the image of God operative in their lives and consider, if need be, first steps on another way. After the 11:15 a.m. mass at which I preached these thoughts, a parishioner thanked me for setting in front of her a theology quiz. Because she seemed to mean a moral, spiritual, practical quiz—not just a theoretical one—I felt affirmed in what I was trying to do.

An email exchange with a regular participant in the Tuesday lunchtime brown bag lectionary study at school proved instrumental in finalizing my sermon preparation. It was there that the links between the "in whom we live and move and have our being" and the process theology tools in my kit got looped back to Paul's initial words to the Athenians about an *unknown* God.[11]

---

8. M. L. Taylor and Berry, *Loving Yourself*, 80.
9. M. L. Taylor and Berry, *Loving Yourself*, 82–83.
10. M. L. Taylor and Berry, *Loving Yourself*, 84–87 and 92–96.
11. Karyn Frazier, email to author, May 19, 2017.

"To an Unknown God in Whom We Live and Move and Have Our Being"
The Sixth Sunday of Easter
Acts 17:22–31; Psalm 66:7–18; 1 Peter 3:13–22; John 14:15–21
May 21, 2017

Last Sunday night, my wife Debra and I sat down to watch a film called *The Founder*.[12] Consider this your spoiler alert! The movie tells the origin story of the McDonald's fast-food empire back in the 1950s and early 60s. Debra and I sat down to watch a film about a pervasive, if ambiguous, icon of American popular culture. But you never know what you're going to get. We couldn't sleep after watching *The Founder*. We just had to talk about the theological question raised by a seemingly simple story of American life and values: where is God in all this? That question still nagged at us on Monday, and we kept talking. On Tuesday, I had to research a little the true story upon which the film is based.[13] Debra and I had sat down to watch a movie about a chain of restaurants serving hamburgers and French fries but got, unknowingly, a theological quiz about God's presence and activity in relation to human greed and cruelty and disdain for the truth. Where is God when a person loses something they have poured their heart into? And where is God when someone plunders something held in another person's heart?

For you see, "founder" in the movie's title refers not to Mac and Dick McDonald but to a man named Ray Kroc. The McDonald brothers operated a few restaurants in southern California and came up with a revolutionary process and commercial kitchen design for serving food fast, faster, fastest, without dining room or tables and chairs or plates and cutlery. Ray Kroc was a mediocre traveling salesman who stumbled on to the McDonalds and connived and pestered them into contracting with him to franchise and expand their ideas and practices. Then Ray Kroc realized the *real* money was in *real estate*, not food. Soon enough, the McDonalds' commitment to quality and to people posed a barrier to Kroc's ambition. He broke the original contract and bought the brothers out—paying them just a tiny fraction of what his McDonald's Corporation would eventually be worth—even making off with the rights to market their family name.

---

12. Hancock, dir., *The Founder*.
13. Brancaccio, "True Origin Story."

So Fill Our Imaginations

Driving around the Midwest in the late 1950s, Ray Kroc noticed that every decent-sized town had a church adorned with a cross and a courthouse flying an American flag. He imagined adding a third landmark—on land *he* owned—taking Dick McDonald's drawing of a little sloped roof, glass-fronted restaurant with arches on either side that together traced the letter *m*. And so, between the cross and the Stars and Stripes, Ray Kroc built the golden arches.

૭ ૨

The book of Acts places the apostle Paul between cultures and their religious wisdoms. Between the familiarity and homogeneity of the Jewish synagogue and the strange, public diversity of the Greco-Roman marketplace. Between strict adherence to one God and numerous temples to a teeming pantheon of gods and goddesses. In every new Greek city he enters, Paul goes first to the synagogue to share his good news with fellow Jews. Some believe; others don't. The issue that divides them is whether a crucified and risen man, Jesus, could really be God's Messiah. Then Paul turns to the gentiles with the same gospel and garners similar mixed results. Some Greeks accept his message, especially the leading women of the city. However, Paul's gospel also causes an uproar in the marketplace, especially among the leading men, who accuse him of turning the political and economic world upside down by announcing a new king, other than and different from the Roman emperor—Christ crucified and risen. Because of his gospel, Paul often ends up in a third place—before a council of some sort—to be interrogated and then imprisoned or beaten or spirited out of town by allies. When he moves on to another Greek city, the cycle begins all over again.

This morning's reading finds Paul in Athens—the capital city of Greek wisdom. He's been to the synagogue. He's been to the marketplace. Now he's invited to the Areopagus to share his teaching with a group of Epicurean and Stoic philosophers. "Athenians," Paul addresses the assembled lovers of wisdom, "I see how extremely religious you are in every way. For as I went through the city and looked carefully at the objects of your worship, I found among them an altar with the inscription, 'To an unknown god'" (Acts 17:22–23). In the words that follow, Paul's voice is often heard as chastising: he knows something the Athenians don't know about God, and he's going to set their theology straight. To be sure, speaking out of his Jewish worldview, Paul is troubled by physical representations of the

To an Unknown God in Whom We Live and Move and Have Our Being

divine in gold or silver or stone and by the notion that God might live in shrines made by human hands and be fed by their sacrificial offerings. But this morning, I hear Paul genuinely appreciating and embracing something from Greek wisdom concerning God. After all, he goes on to quote two Greek philosopher-poets to make his point.

I wonder if the open-ended and imageless altar Paul finds—not to *this* particular god or *that* one but to an *unknown* god—grants spaciousness around any human attempt to define God too tightly or too rightly. What if the altar's inscription testifies to a God always beyond our capacity to know or imagine fully, and thereby to try to manipulate or possess? I even wonder if Paul finds in the wisdom of the Greeks a corrective to his own people's tendency to think of the one God as a tribal god, the god of a single people, their people. Paul's language in Athens is about *all*, rather than *some* or *a few*. "God gives to *all* mortals life and breath and *all* things," he says. "From one ancestor God made *all* nations to inhabit the *whole* earth, and God allotted the times of their existence and the boundaries of the places where they would live, so that they would search for God . . . and find God—though indeed God is not far from *each one* of us" (Acts 17:25–27). That is why no one altar to any known god is ever big enough or right enough.

How could such a spacious, unknown god be far from us if "in God we live and move and have our being"? Borrowing this line from Epimenides, an ancient Athenian poet, Paul weaves together the best of Greek wisdom with his own Jewish heritage (Acts 17:28). And Paul offers to turn our Christian image of God inside out as well.

What a paradigm shift! Instead of God *in the world* or *in us*, we live *in God* and have our being *in God*. Encompassed by God, pervaded by God. God the air within which we have air to breathe, the water within which we find water. God above us and beyond us and in us, only because we first live and have our being in God. We can only be far from what is outside us and separate from us. But if we are *within* God, then God is closer to us than we are to ourselves. In God we live and have our being. All of us, not some, not a few. *All*. We do not possess the life and breath and all things God gives to all mortals; they always already surround us—we find ourselves immersed in them, and so we merely borrow them. The times of our existence spread out within God. The places where we dwell are small dots of sacred ground within the landscape that is God.

In God we live and have our being. We also *move* in God, move as we might move through air or water. God's presence does not resist us, as if we were two solid objects trying to occupy the same space. It's not a choice between either God or us present—but both at once. In God we move as we choose: for good and for ill. Within God we can move out toward connection with all who live and move and have their being in God, or we can clench down into ourselves or into little eddies of some or a few. And God does not resist, at least not as some superhero would. Instead, God continues to encompass and pervade, give life and breath and all things. The God in whom we move is a more pervasive God but also more vulnerable.

The most apt analogy for this theological paradigm shift might be the child in her mother's womb. The child encompassed and pervaded by the water of the mother's womb. The child floating in the mother, breathing her, fed by and with the mother's own substance and nothing else. The mother the only environment, the only universe, the child knows—life and breath and all things. And the child moves within the mother—without meeting coercive resistance—the child is given space within the mother to grow and develop. Which is why the God in whom we live and move and have our being is unknown, why no altar is ever big or right enough. Not because God is distant, but because God is so close. Like the child within the mother, we cannot get enough distance on God to experience God as separate or outside. "Our Savior is our true Mother," Julian of Norwich once wrote, "in whom we are endlessly born and out of whom we shall never come."[14]

So maybe the unavoidable question—where is God in all this?—needs to be reframed, at least on this one Sunday morning with Paul's words to the Athenians as one of our Scripture readings. Not where is God in our lives and our world, but where are we in God? How are we in God? What are we up to within God? How do we live and move and have our being? Spaciously? Open to all others who are also within God (which means all others!)? Or clenched around some or a few or ourselves?

෴

As *The Founder* tells it, when Ray Kroc breaks his contract in order to buy out Mac and Dick McDonald, he also informs his wife Ethel—at the dinner table—that he's filing for divorce. Ray wants to be with Joan, wife of one of his franchise owners, instead. In real life, it took years for Joan to end up with Ray—so much so that Ray married another woman in the interim, only to divorce her when Joan became available. Eventually, Ray and Joan married, lived together, and the McDonald's fortune passed to Joan Kroc

---

14. Julian of Norwich, *Showings*, 292.

To an Unknown God in Whom We Live and Move and Have Our Being

after Ray's death. And what did she do with it? Joan Kroc gave it away, gave it all away—often piecemeal and anonymously, in reaction to stories in the news. Joan Kroc's two large public bequests were to the Salvation Army and National Public Radio. Did Joan Kroc's gifts compensate the McDonald brothers for their losses? No, not in any direct way. Was Ray Kroc punished for his greed and cruelty and disdain for the truth; did he live in a hell of his own making the last years of his life? I don't know, but I doubt it. This I do believe, the God in whom all live and move and have their being draws on the generosity of Joan Kroc and that of many others, puts it to use, in myriad unknown ways, recirculating life-giving resources throughout the vast, universal womb that is God.

It's not that I never launch sermons from, or land them in, my own personal experience. I do. I tell stories from my life. I listen to others who preach that way. I love the way Helen Roll began a 5:00 p.m. shared homily at St. Paul's on the story of the Israelites complaining about their food in the wilderness as they wandered between liberation and promised land by saying, "I am a complainer." I've even chaired a doctor of ministry project on autobiographical preaching.[15]

In fact, some of my recent sermons feel *more* autobiographical, more directly imaging my own experience, than these twelve. I wonder . . . No, I *believe* this arises out of living with my dad's late-onset Alzheimer's.[16] My wife's journey through breast cancer surgery and radiation, and the predominantly non-white community of health care workers and fellow patients and family members and friends into which we were welcomed at Seattle's Swedish Cancer Institute.[17] And my mom's death a couple of years ago, on the eve of the Fourth Sunday of Advent, after a short bout with cancer. People called her Betty, but her name was Elizabeth. The very first Sunday Gospel reading I heard after her death, sitting in the pews at St. Paul's, was Luke 1:39–45: the story of Mary's visit to her cousin Elizabeth

---

15. Parker, "Preaching to Belong."
16. See M. L. Taylor, "Making Room for Others."
17. See M. L. Taylor, "Blessed Are Who?"

and how the baby in Elizabeth's womb leaped for joy at Mary's greeting and the coming of Jesus.[18]

That sort of autobiographical preaching, however, does not represent my only or default setting. I also try to get real, try to get experiential with the listening congregation, through movies or novels or other works of art. The storyline of a movie, as above in the sermon "To an Unknown God in Whom We Live and Move and Have Our Being." Or a scene from a movie. A single image. I readily admit that the image of the golden arches of McDonald's between the cross and the Stars and Stripes suggested by the movie *The Founder* contained a surplus of meaning well beyond the film's storyline and the God-issues it raised for me, which I tried to address in my preaching. A surplus of meaning well beyond my attempt to locate the Paul of Acts 17 between synagogue and marketplace, as I transitioned from the first to the second move of the sermon. But as did others, my sixth sermon from the 2016–2017 church year exercised subsequent agency. More later, in the conclusion to this book.

---

18. See M. L. Taylor, "Watching Over."

7

Compassion: Visceral, Face-to-Face and Hands-On, Limitlessly Expansive

[Remarks for Shared Homily]

The Second Sunday after Pentecost

IN OVER TWENTY YEARS now, I have only once *not* preached from a full, written manuscript at morning masses at St. Paul's. I believe it was my very first homily at the parish. The Gospel that Sunday was the third of Jesus' "predictions" of his passion from Mark (10:32–45), which ends with the line, "For the Son of Man came not to be served (*diakonēthēnai*) but to serve (*diakonēsai*), and to give his life a ransom for many." From a written outline of points, I tried to develop the notion of Jesus (and us all) as deacon, tracing through Mark's Gospel the various characters who serve or wait on others. The angels with Jesus in the wilderness (Mark 1:12–13). Simon Peter's mother-in-law after Jesus "lifted her up" and healed her of her fever (Mark 1:31). The Galilean women who followed Jesus to Jerusalem and were present at his crucifixion, including Mary Magdalene, Mary the mother of James, and Salome (Mark 15:40–41). And Jesus, again, who says to the Twelve in Mark 9:35: "Whoever wants to be first must be last of all and servant (*diakonos*) of all." I still use a photocopy of my outline for that sermon when I teach the Gospel of Mark, because it lists out all those texts containing the deacon words.

People at St. Paul's expect morning sermons to be delivered orally with success on Sunday and then be suitable for posting on the parish website as written texts by Tuesday or so. Maybe I should feel more flattered when folk greet me in the entryway after a morning service at which I have preached and ask if they could get a written copy of the sermon or if it will be available on the website. Flattered that they want to hold on to my words and continue to mull them over. But I don't! I worry instead that my preaching from the pulpit was too literary in character to be "heard." Recently—well after the morning sermons in this book were delivered—I have tried to address this self-perceived shortcoming by writing and preaching from a manuscript that looks visually more like a script for an actor in a play, with discreet oral phrases or units set as separate lines and with extra hard returns or even page breaks to indicate endings and transitions. I now convert the Sunday morning oral script to sentences and paragraphs with proper punctuation and indentation and formatting only on Mondays or Tuesdays.

Preaching—or should I say, facilitating the shared homily—on Sunday evenings is different. I do sometimes preach from a written manuscript at 5:00 p.m. Often, literally, a *manu*-script—handwritten, not typed, which is how I do all my real sermon composition anyway. But I have also preached in the evening with just the Gospel or lectionary book open on my lap. No manuscript of any sort, no outline, no notes. I love the freedom that strategy offers to make lots of eye contact with worshippers seated around me in a circle, some just a few feet away. Most of the time, however, I am too insecure in my abilities to try to preach without some written cues in front of me. Without a script, I forget things. I get confused. I ramble. And so I often employ a written outline when preaching at the evening service. This was the case with my remarks on June 18, 2017, the Second Sunday after Pentecost. In what follows, you will find a slightly cleaned up and typed version of what was my handwritten outline on the occasion.

"Compassion: Visceral, Face-to-Face and Hands-On, Limitlessly Expansive"
[Remarks for Shared Homily]
The Second Sunday after Pentecost; Proper 6A
Exodus 19:2–8a; Psalm 100; Romans 5:1–8; Matthew 9:35—10:8
June 18, 2017

Compassion: Visceral, Face-to-Face and Hands-On, Limitlessly Expansive

1)

- Gospel of Matthew—paging back in the book to what we skipped over between First Sunday in Lent and Trinity Sunday last week;
- tonight: the beginning of Jesus' Galilean ministry and the naming/sending of the twelve apostles
- stories of *the compassion of Jesus*:
    - *visceral, face-to-face and hands-on, limitlessly expansive* compassion

2a)

- compassion—*splagchnizomai* (entrails, guts); compassion of Jesus not theoretical but visceral

2b)

- Jesus' guts moved by face-to-face and hands-on encounter; he went about *all* the cities and villages, curing *every* sickness and disease
    - in Matthew's telling: leper cleansed; centurion's slave healed; Peter's mother-in-law and all possessed by demons in her town; demons cast out of two men living among the tombs; then still more healings—a paralytic, synagogue leader's daughter raised from the dead, woman with the hemorrhages, two blind men, and a man rendered mute by a demon
- the harvest is plentiful—a backwards harvest, not of gathering in but of giving away; a harvest of compassion

2c)

- once moved in his guts by all this face-to-face and hands-on encounter, Jesus begins to see more broadly, and his compassion begins to expand and spread and spread out to touch more and more need
- not enough Jesus to go around, so the Twelve are given instructions to do what Jesus has been doing: cure the sick, raise the dead, cleanse lepers, cast out demons

So Fill Our Imaginations

- not enough Jesus to go around, so his mission of proclaiming the good news enlists allies, additional Christs—first the Twelve, then Mary Magdalene, eventually our own apostle Paul
- at first, Jesus warns the Twelve to go nowhere among the gentiles and enter no town of the Samaritans; but later in Matthew, Jesus himself goes to Tyre and Sidon and casts out a demon; in Luke's Gospel, the parable of the *good* Samaritan; in John, Jesus with the Samaritan woman at the well, then accused of being a demon-possessed Samaritan himself
- you received without payment, give without payment

3)

- on Wednesday—after brainstorming these thoughts about the compassion of Jesus—these three news stories in the space of fifteen minutes: the shooting at the Republican Party baseball practice by a Bernie Sanders supporter, the fire in the twenty-one-story apartment building in London after months and months of complaints about lack of safety, and the sudden withdrawal of the lawsuit against Seattle's mayor for sexual abuse

4)

- Which causes me to wonder, what holds us back from visceral, face-to-face and hands'-on compassion?
- I wonder what keeps our compassion from expanding limitlessly to touch any and all need?
- And I wonder when you have reached out in compassion or been touched by compassion from another?
- I invite . . .

I must say, of the twelve, I was least satisfied with this sermon after having delivered it. I liked my core insight of Jesus' compassion as visceral, face-to-face and hands-on, and limitlessly expansive.[1] But it feels like there's

1. Suggested by Albert Nolan's discussion of *splagchnizomai* (compassion) and *splagchnon* (entrails) in *Jesus before Christianity*, 34–35.

Compassion: Visceral, Face-to-Face and Hands-On, Limitlessly Expansive

too much going on. Too many moving parts. And even as I delivered my remarks from the handwritten outline that Sunday evening, I found myself wishing I had done more with (or maybe made focal) the idea of a reverse or backwards harvest of giving away rather than gathering in.

I know this raises all sorts of questions about the purpose of preaching and what might constitute success or failure. I'm hesitant to offer any normative or prescriptive answers. (For better or for worse, there's an indirectness not just to my preaching but to my theological reflection upon preaching!) A few descriptive on-ramps will have to suffice.

I remember Joe Williamson, senior pastor at Boston's Church of the Covenant, that federated UCC/PC(USA) congregation I attended in the 1980s, saying that preaching at its best brings together the personhood of the preacher, the life of the congregation, and the message of Scripture. That's not bad.

A perennial challenge, as an occasional preacher whose day job is that of theology professor, lies in managing the differences between pulpit and classroom. And the multiple feedback loops between them. I became an academic theologian in the first place because of what was going on with my faith, its life-empowerment as well as life-challenges, with what was going on in and around church. And my teaching at school aims to help equip people for competent and resilient leadership in churches and for spiritually-infused leadership in non-ecclesial places. So, what I do now at church, including preaching, consistently makes its way into my classes. To top it all off, I quickly and unexpectedly discovered that preaching downstairs at 5:00 p.m. on Sundays at St. Paul's feels more like my Monday through Friday teaching than does being in the pulpit upstairs on Sunday morning. For better or worse, my style is to teach *alongside* my students, rather than from *in front* of them. I rarely lecture in the classroom. I present theological artifacts and critical incidents and pose questions. I lead discussions. Discussions about what my students feel, think, do, and "be." Which is more like facilitating a *shared* homily on Sunday evening in that Godly Play-like, Montessori-esque circle of folk already with their own legitimate and valuable experience and insights. I feel more myself, preaching around the altar and across from one another in that circle, than I do alone and elevated in that ship-prow pulpit, however beautiful and suggestive of other values.

Another challenge also comes with being both an occasional preacher and regular professor: time. I have the luxury of pouring too much time into sermon composition, for it feels perilously akin to the theologizing I do for

So Fill Our Imaginations

my classes. I need to fight that tendency in order to attend to other less enthralling responsibilities at school. Nevertheless, as I reflect upon the preceding sermon, I am struck that if I had spent just a little more time with it, my preaching would have been more concise, more direct, less diffuse. Better.

One final descriptive comment on the purpose of preaching, its success or failure. As in all human meaning-making, preaching occurs *between* the preacher's composition and delivery and the congregation's reception—not in either one alone. As well as *beyond*, in the subsequent agency of a sermon. So, even if of the twelve I felt least satisfied with the remarks for shared homily you just read, such dissatisfaction is not the sole indicator of success or failure.

8

Let Both of Them Grow Together until the Harvest

[Remarks for Shared Homily]

The Seventh Sunday after Pentecost

THE GODLY PLAY CURRICULUM consists of an ever-growing set of lesson series. Four lessons for Advent[1]—no surprise there. An eight-lesson series on the great stories of God's people from the Hebrew Testament of Christian Scripture: creation, the flood and Noah's ark, the exodus, the ark of the covenant and the temple, exile and return.[2] All (ideally) involving wooden figurines of people and structures and animals. Many set in the ever-popular "desert box" full of sand. There's a series called "Faces of Easter," which uses plaques with drawings of faces on them to tell the life of Jesus from infancy to baptism and temptation, adult work and words, then Last Supper, Christ crucified and risen.[3]

The Godly Play lessons on the parables of Jesus all come in golden, lidded, wooden boxes containing materials with which to retell the parables.[4] Sheep, shepherd, and wolf (good shepherd). Seeds and rocks and birds and good soil (sower). A great pearl. But the parable lessons begin with

---

1. Berryman, *Complete Guide*, 3:27–51.
2. Berryman, *Complete Guide*, 2:41–99.
3. Berryman, *Complete Guide*, 4:32–68.
4. Berryman, *Complete Guide*, 3:77–120.

attention to, and wondering about, the golden boxes themselves—the nature of, gift and challenge associated with, parables.

The Gospel for the Seventh Sunday after Pentecost (July 23, 2017) was Jesus' parable of the weeds among the wheat from Matthew 13. I launched my remarks that evening with one of the Godly Play parable boxes beside me on the floor and used a version of the preparatory actions and words around the parabolic form. But the box itself was empty, except for a sheet of paper with the text of Matthew 13:24–30 printed on it, because the weeds among the wheat is not one of the six parables of Jesus included within the Godly Play curriculum. And to keep our wondering about this parable as playful and open-ended as possible I intentionally avoided any mention at all of Matthew's allegorical interpretation of the parable, later, in verses 36–43 of chapter 13—the second half of the lectionary's appointed Gospel reading.

Working on a parable of Jesus with adults as if we were children in a Godly Play classroom so filled my imagination that I came away from this sermon with the urge to create a "real" Godly Play lesson on the parable of the weeds among the wheat. You'll find the lesson Melissa Trull and I cowrote in the conclusion to this book, along with commentary about our creative process.

The following remarks for shared homily touched on the intertwined local social/political/economic issues of housing (increasingly unaffordable), upzoning (larger, taller buildings in older residential neighborhoods providing a much more densely packed city population—of those affluent enough to afford to live in Seattle), and encampments of unsheltered folk living on the sidewalks and parking strips of Seattle. I described these issues for you back in the introduction. I also had in my mind's eye the horrific television images of the utter destruction of Mosul, Iraq, and Homs, Syria, by the U.S. and its allies and the Russians with theirs, all in the name of liberating those now nonexistent cities from occupation by the Islamic State Group.

Let Both of Them Grow Together until the Harvest

"Let Both of Them Grow Together until the Harvest"
[Remarks for Shared Homily]
The Seventh Sunday after Pentecost; Proper 11A
Isaiah 44:6–8; Psalm 86:11–17; Romans 8:12–25; Matthew 13:24–30, 36–43
July 23, 2017

The Godly Play curriculum in which the children of St. Paul's engage includes a series of lessons on the parables of Jesus. The parable of the weeds among the wheat from this evening's Gospel reading is not one of them, but play along with me a little.

MOVEMENTS	WORDS
Pick the parable up from the floor and place it on your lap to wonder about the box and its contents.	Now let's see. The box is the color gold. Something valuable must be inside. Parables are very valuable, even more important than gold, so maybe there is a parable inside.
Raise the box and extend it as if offering it to the circle of people sharing the homily.	The box looks kind of like a present. Parables are like presents. They were given to you even before you were born. They are yours. You don't need to take them. They are already yours, even if you don't know what they are.
Press the fingers of one hand against the lid of the box, trying to get inside. Then turn the box around this way and that, still focusing on the lid.	The box has a lid. It stops us. You see, sometimes, even if we are really ready, it can be hard to go inside a parable. They are just like that. I don't know why. Don't be discouraged if you can't find your way in. Keep coming back, and one day the parable will open up for you.
Take off the lid and show the circle of people that the box is empty . . . *. . . except for a sheet of paper with the text of Matthew 13:24–30 printed out.*	I have an idea. Let's see what is inside the box. Maybe there is a parable inside. Oh no, I have some bad news! There is nothing in the box to help us get ready for the parable. All we can do is just begin again with the words we've already heard in our Gospel reading.

So Fill Our Imaginations

MOVEMENTS	WORDS

If this had been a real Godly Play parable lesson, inside the box there might have been a brown cloth underlay for the field, figures of a sower and an enemy with seeds, wheat plants and weeds all grown up together, and a bundle of weeds and a barn full of wheat.

Jesus put before the crowd another parable:

> The kingdom of heaven may be compared to someone who sowed good seed in his field; but while everybody was asleep, an enemy came and sowed weeds among the wheat. So when the plants came up and bore grain, the weeds appeared as well. And the slaves of the householder came and said, "Master, did you not sow good seed in your field? Where, then, did these weeds come from?" He answered, "An enemy has done this." The slaves said to him, "Then do you want us to go and gather them?" But he replied, "No; for in gathering the weeds you would uproot the wheat along with them. Let both of them grow together until the harvest; and at harvest time I will tell the reapers, Collect the weeds first and bind them in bundles to be burned, but gather the wheat into my barn."

Something dramatic changes—as if overnight—but no one notices until it's too late. The weeds are not good; it is not right that they are in the field along with the good seed. An enemy is responsible. There is no excusing or ignoring the real evil of the situation. This is *not* the way it's supposed to be.

But what to do? Should we go and deal with the weeds, with what is not supposed to be, by removing it, uprooting it? No, if you do that, if you go out to uproot evil forcefully, you will destroy the good as well. *Let both of them grow together until the harvest.* Then there will be a separation—but not of your doing.

This evening, I find myself entering the parable of the weeds among the wheat in two ways.

First, at a very local, Seattle level, on the day after I cast my primary election ballot, like the slaves of the landowner, I am shocked to see weeds growing where good seed was planted. Something is not right. Something dramatic has changed—as if overnight—and I didn't notice until it was too late. A little bungalow in my neighborhood gets torn down, and a huge multiunit building has gone up. A series of homeless minicamps has sprung up—not under Interstate 5 where I never had to look at them—but just outside this church building on First Avenue North. An apartment building gets sold out from under members of this parish, and the members move out of the city. More and more people of color and immigrants and families with children leave Seattle for Kent or Renton or farther out.

Second, at a national and international level, leaders want to shake up politics as usual but threaten to destroy the very political household we inhabit. Military coalitions liberate large, ancient cities from their enemies by utterly destroying those cities.

Let both of them grow together until the harvest.

Some of Jesus' parables call to decisive action, right here and now. This parable is different. It invites patient hope, hopeful patience.

Our reading from Paul's Letter to the Romans wraps additional words around Jesus' parable of the weeds among the wheat. The creation—subject to futility—waits with eager longing to be set free from bondage and decay. The whole creation has been groaning with labor pains; we groan while we wait for adoption. In hope we are saved. But hope that is seen is not hope. For who hopes for what is seen? But if we hope for what we do not see, we wait for it with patience. Maybe this is because of how powerfully our sense of sight directs our experience. Maybe our other senses—touching and hearing and tasting and smelling—are especially important as we learn to hope, to wait with patience.

I remember sitting on the couch with my daughter Rebekah in Minnesota after the surgery to address her brain aneurysm. Neither of us could see what would happen next. All we could do was hold one another. Touching. Waiting. Hoping.

I wonder how you're doing with the lid on the box that contains the parable of the weeds among the wheat?

I wonder when you have needed to let both of them grow together until the harvest?

And I wonder, as you hope for what you do not see, if touching or hearing or tasting or smelling helps you wait with patience?

I invite . . .

So Fill Our Imaginations

Let's follow two threads of reflection coming out of these remarks for shared homily.

First, Kierkegaard. You've been waiting for his cameo appearance, haven't you? Well, here it is.

Søren Kierkegaard (1813–1855)—Danish theologian? philosopher? poet? novelist? literary critic? reformer of the church?—never married and never had children of his own. He was engaged to Regine Olsen but broke off the engagement after a year, a month, and a day. Kierkegaard never really held a job, even though he possessed all the education and formation to enter one of two professions. He could have become either a university professor or a pastor in the Danish Lutheran Church. He chose *not* to pursue an academic appointment. He chose *not* to seek ordination. Instead, instead of starting a family and taking up a profession, and living mostly on wealth he inherited from his father, Kierkegaard poured himself into a staggeringly intense and meteoric career as an author, producing over thirty books in just twelve years.

Some of Kierkegaard's works are quite brief—little pamphlets, really. Others are prodigiously long. Half a dozen exceed three hundred pages in length, each. The longest falls a single page short of eight hundred in English translation. Many of their title pages—especially the shorter and more explicitly religious ones—bear the name S. Kierkegaard as author. But in other books, Kierkegaard practices what he called "indirect communication," writing under a riotous collection of pseudonyms: Hilarius Bookbinder; Nicholas Notabene; Inter et Inter; first Johannes Climacus; then, later on, Anti-Climacus. Earnestness and jest collide. One Vigilius Haufniensis (the watchperson of Copenhagen) writes an erudite, even pedantic, treatise on original sin, while a book entitled *Repetition* comes from the pen of the whimsically named Constantin Constantius. A pseudonymous author appends a six-hundred-page postscript to an original work of just a hundred pages. Another book consists solely of eight prefaces (nine, counting the book's own), because the pseudonym's wife refuses to allow him to disrupt their domestic routine by writing a complete book.

The very first book in the authorship, a huge two-volume work called *Either/Or*, epitomizes Kierkegaard's strategy of indirectness. Edited by Victor Eremita (the "victorious hermit"), *Either/Or* purportedly contains the papers of two different authors, A and B, whose manuscripts Eremita claims to have discovered by accident in a secret compartment behind a hidden panel of an old desk purchased at a secondhand shop.⁵ A's motley collection of aesthetic pieces (imaginative, pathos-filled aphorisms, along with essays and addresses on everything from Mozart's operas to the "silhouettes" of three women in literature deceived by their male lovers) makes up volume 1 of *Either/Or*, the "either"; except that, mirroring Eremita's reticence, A disavows being the author of its final and longest component, the diary of a seducer named Johannes, claiming instead merely to have edited it.⁶ Volume 2, the "or," consists of two massive, didactic letters from B (a judge named William), addressed to A, written on lined legal paper, telling the younger man to get serious with his life and stop playing around.⁷ The adequacy of the judge's ethical standpoint, as well as the very binary construct of either/or, however, are called into question by a country pastor's sermon with which the second volume of *Either/Or* ends.⁸ The sermon extols the good news that, in relation to God, we human beings are all always in the wrong.

But why pseudonyms? Why such indirect communication? Many scholars have wrestled with these intriguing, maddening questions for many years. For the purposes of this (my) book, I advance just one claim. Pseudonymity was not designed to hide Kierkegaard's ultimate responsibility for the books. Everyone in Denmark knew almost immediately that they belonged to him. Indeed, the name S. Kierkegaard appears on the title pages of many of the pseudonymous writings as editor. Rather, the indirectness of Kierkegaard's authorship relates essentially to the topics he takes up. Kierkegaard seems to have believed that truth, existential truth, truth concerning human life, human values, human meaning, could not be communicated objectively and directly by one person to another, transferred from one person's mind and heart to another's. On the contrary, existential truth must be engaged, enacted, subjectively or personally, with intentionality and passion by each human being in the living of their life. The most a writer or a teacher (a parent or a preacher?) can do is to offer the student or reader (hearer or child?) images, possibilities, life options, which they might then try on for themselves. So, Kierkegaard creates pseudonyms, fictional authors, with their own life-views—be they aesthetic, ethical, or religious—which they embody and for which they speak each in their own distinctive voice, independent of whether Søren Kierkegaard himself actually believed

---

5. Kierkegaard, *Either/Or, Part I*, 3:3–15.
6. Kierkegaard, *Either/Or, Part I*, 3:17–445.
7. Kierkegaard, *Either/Or, Part II*, 4:3–333.
8. Kierkegaard, *Either/Or, Part II*, 4:335–54.

such things or lived them out. The goal of this exercise is for the reader, having weighed the insights and inadequacies of both a Johannes the Seducer and a Judge William, to come to some decision about how they will now live.

With the glaring exception of a series of newspaper articles and tracts from the last year of his life savagely and satirically attacking the Danish church, its clergy and bishops, a nondirective stance also characterizes the works directly signed S. Kierkegaard. Like the pseudonymous books, they invite an active, participatory response from the reader, whether in edifying discourses on patience, which require the reader to develop and practice that very virtue in order to work their way through Kierkegaard's words,[9] or communion discourses about the women in the Gospels who anoint Jesus and whose stories Kierkegaard uses to query the reader, gently, concerning their need for shelter and nurture as they come forward to receive the body and blood of Jesus Christ in the sacrament of the altar.[10]

I believe Kierkegaard's strategy of indirect communication anticipates Montessori educational principles, generally, and Jerome Berryman's Godly Play, particularly. In an open classroom, the teacher does not tell the child what to think or who to be. They strive, rather, to create a safe and boundaried, while rich and challenging, environment in which children make their own meaning, learn for themselves, and grow. With an indirectness Kierkegaard might applaud, Berryman often abstains from using the name "Jesus" in his Godly Play lessons, even his most christological ones, instead allowing the *how* of praxis to define the *what* or *who* of identity. Frequently, the curriculum employs locutions such as "the baby" or "the boy" or "the Good Shepherd." Never naming him explicitly, the parable lessons introduce Jesus this way: "There was once someone who did such amazing things and said such wonderful things that people followed him," often with this transition to the parable itself: "As they followed him, they heard him speaking about a kingdom. The kingdom was not like the one they were in. It was not like one that anyone had ever visited. It was not like any kingdom anyone had even heard about. So they had to ask him, 'What is the kingdom of [God] like?'"[11] This restraint around the name of Jesus has the effect of inviting children to wonder, and also wander a bit, daring them to discover the good shepherd or someone who did and said amazing, wonderful things

---

9. Kierkegaard, *Eighteen Upbuilding Discourses*, 159–75, 181–203.

10. Kierkegaard, *Without Authority*, 135–88. For a discussion of these discourses and their Gospel women, see my essay "Practice in Authority."

11. See Berryman, *Complete Guide*, 4:105, for example.

in unexpected places in their lives and in the world. Those golden, lidded boxes in which the parable lessons come augment Godly Play's indirectness. More Kierkegaardian still is a Lenten lesson in which Jesus, the one who told parables, eventually realized he had to become a parable himself and so turned toward Jerusalem for the last time, to die.[12]

As an educator, I detect the murmurings of both outer and inner resistance to the notion that the indirectness of an open Montessori classroom has the capacity to teach justice. Maybe I need to take more to heart the time I was sharing Jesus' parable of the leaven with the first- to third-grade Godly Play group at St. Paul's and asked, "I wonder if you have ever come close to something little that caused such a big change, I mean, in your life?" A child replied: "Human beings. We're so small, but with global warming, we've caused big changes to the earth." Maybe I need to become more confident in getting the materials right, the ones to be placed at the center of the circle to prompt and carry lessons aimed at calling forth justice from children or adults, and then, even more important, getting the questions right, the wondering questions for such lessons.

As a scholar of Kierkegaard's writings, I continue to ask: can authorial indirection serve as a social/political/economic strategy of resistance and advocacy, or does it always remain supportive of the status quo from a safe distance of privilege? Must we follow Kierkegaard at the end of his life in abandoning indirectness for polemical attack? These questions were top of my mind whilst I taught my Kierkegaard seminar at school last winter.

And as an author myself, I wonder if you'll conclude that the indirectness of my preaching and my theological reflection upon preaching is for better or for worse? I invite you to let me know. Thank you!

The second thread: an unforgettable class during my graduate work in theological studies, unforgettable because the professor turned us loose to pursue real research, was a seminar on the idea of religious toleration among the Reformers of the sixteenth century. Roman Catholic, Anglican, and Protestant Reformers. It was a doctoral seminar, and you had to have a working grasp of one of the original languages used by the sixteenth-century reformers to gain entry. (I thought those who opted to read Sir Thomas More in English got off easy!) A couple of church history students had Latin, of course. But it turned out the "low" German in which some of the radical Reformers wrote (think Mennonites and their kin) strongly

---

12. I refer you again to the essay "Playing with Pictures," which Alissabeth Newton and I cowrote.

resembles modern Afrikaans, so I had a pair of black South African classmates. I was just a master's student but with firm plans to go on for doctoral studies. I found I could read John Calvin's sermons in his sixteenth-century French, and so I was in. The French language had not yet developed all its accent marks, the circumflex, and the cedilla. It took me a little while to get used to a word like *desias* all over the pages of the library's *Corpus Reformatorum*—*déjà* in modern French.

Our professor—editing a book on religious toleration during the Reformation, hence the seminar in the first place—was overjoyed when we students discovered (or confirmed) for him that all the early sixteenth-century writers had something to say about the parable of the weeds among the wheat and were quite comfortable applying Jesus' words directly to their situation of new and troubling theological pluralism. Some wanted to line up behind the angels in Matthew's allegorical interpretation and go to work separating weeds (heretics) from wheat (the orthodox)—including Calvin, the guy whose sermons on the book of Deuteronomy I worked with. Others gravitated strongly to the line by the householder in the parable itself, "No [do *not* go and gather them]; for in gathering the weeds you would uproot the wheat along with them." That was the approach of those radical Reformers, persecuted as heretics by Calvinists, Lutherans, Church of England folk, and Roman Catholics. I still get chills recalling the painful gift of reading those radical Reformers in an American graduate school across the table from two black South Africans years before the release of Nelson Mandela from prison and the end of apartheid.

9

The Conversion of Jesus
The Eleventh Sunday after Pentecost

A YEAR OF PREACHING! And this sermon was my favorite in terms of composition and delivery, reception and subsequent agency. It felt both more playful and more national-political than others. The earnestness of my exegetical work with Matthew 15:21–28 served and was surpassed by the jest of proposing a new feast day for the church calendar. Politics and liturgics. Work and play. Earnestness and jest. A few of my favorite things.

I associate the story of Jesus and the Canaanite woman with other stories in the Gospels involving nameless women. The hemorrhaging woman (Mark 5), the widow of Nain (Luke 7), and the Samaritan woman at the well (John 4), for example. These stories raise issues of exclusion and inclusion. Men and women. Who talks to whom in public social/political/economic spaces. Touch or not touching. Self-protection, even hiding self, over against being outed by another. Of all these stories, the one of the Canaanite woman and Jesus is probably the most troubling for most modern readers/hearers. I was surprised—against my expectations—to find that Matthew's version of the story amplifies the trouble of Jesus' initial refusal to help and the trouble of the woman's assertive modesty, compared with the version in Mark's Gospel.

Composing this particular sermon spotlighted the intertextuality of them all. The intertextuality of the Gospel readings for Year A (or B or C, for that matter) of the Revised Common Lectionary. The intertextuality—better, if I can create a word, the "inter-practic-ality" of the Christian message. Already, back in my remarks for the shared homily on June 18 (where the

So Fill Our Imaginations

Gospel reading concerned Jesus' sending out the Twelve), I felt compelled to mention the shifting attitudes of Matthew's Jesus toward a ministry of healing/raising the dead/cleansing lepers/casting out demons among the gentiles. Those words of mine anticipated by two months, and prepared for, the story of the Canaanite woman, where I find a decisive, irreversible turning point for Jesus. A month earlier, in my attempt to open the golden box of the parable of the weeds among the wheat, I remarked that although some of Jesus' parables call for decisive action here and now, the weeds among the wheat invites patient hope/hopeful patience. That's because, I believe, much of the wisdom the Christian religious and spiritual heritage bequeaths to us comes in the form of (seeming) opposites juxtaposed. Queered? Death and life. Law and gospel. Grace and works. Lament and thanksgiving. Word and meal. Feasting and fasting. Both-and, not either/or. But rarely does a single Christian text explicitly acknowledge at one and the same time the *both* of the tradition's wisdom. And so how does the poor preacher reach all people in front of (or beside) them in all life situations, without preaching *two* sermons artificially stitched together, when the readings or the liturgical occasion or the world context grab hold of just one component of the both-and? Again, to my surprise, Matthew's story of Jesus and the Canaanite woman seems to embrace a complete both-and. The woman *both* claims her own voice to speak out *and* refuses to respond in kind to words of exclusion and ridicule, thereby inviting deeper solidarity and inclusion.

An anticipatory note about another intertextual matter in the sermon, especially for my non-Episcopalian readers. In addition to the first reading from Scripture, psalm, second reading, and Gospel for each Sunday and holy day of the church year, our lectionary also appoints what we call the collect of the day, or just *the* collect. This is a brief prayer, offered toward the beginning of a mass, that sets out the primary biblical-theological-spiritual theme for a particular liturgical occasion—much the way an overture might introduce a melody early on in a piece of music. Some of the collects were composed new for the Episcopal Church's 1979 prayer book; others go back a thousand or more years in the history of the Christian church. They intend to be fittingly thematic: collects for use at Christmas concern Jesus' birth, of course; those for Easter, his resurrection from the dead. Although the collects come in several structural forms, many are threefold and begin by addressing/naming/praising God in terms of some action or quality of God's; then there's a brief petition asking God to do something in and for us, or to empower our capacity to do something or be someone; finally, a concluding doxology, often Trinitarian. Because of their stereotypical literary shape, the collects have been likened to sonnets or haikus.[1] And while it's the priest presiding at the mass who alone speaks or chants the collect out loud, the notion is that they pray on behalf of the entire assembly, that we all pray the collect collectively. Here's the one appointed for the Sunday closest to August 17, when, in Lectionary Year A, we also hear the story of Jesus and the Canaanite woman.

> Almighty God,
> you have given your only Son to be for us a sacrifice for sin,
> and also an example of godly life:
> Give us grace to receive thankfully the fruits of his redeeming work,
> and to follow daily in the blessed steps of his most holy life;
> through Jesus Christ your Son our Lord,
> who lives and reigns with you and the Holy Spirit,
> one God, now and forever.[2]

"The Conversion of Jesus"
The Eleventh Sunday after Pentecost; Proper 15A
Isaiah 56:1, 6–8; Psalm 67; Romans 11:1–2a, 29–32; Matthew 15:21–28
August 20, 2017

> "Thus says the Lord God, who gathers the outcasts of Israel, I will gather others to them besides those already gathered."
>
> —ISAIAH 56:8

I want to propose an addition to the church calendar this morning, a new feast day. A feast celebrating a moment in the life of Jesus, like the presentation or ascension or transfiguration. This morning, I want to propose the Feast of the Conversion of Our Lord Jesus Christ. For in Matthew's story

---

1. See Hatchett, *Commentary*, 163–65, for a general discussion of the form and function of the collects; then 165–216, for historical information on each of the over 120 individual collects in the prayer book.
2. Episcopal Church, *Book of Common Prayer*, 232.

of Jesus and the Canaanite woman, we have the perfect Gospel reading for such a new feast day.

Conversion. Being turned around. Having one's mind or outlook on life changed. Radical transformation. We don't usually associate such words with Jesus. But if we adhere to our creeds and take the full humanity of Jesus every bit as seriously as his true divinity, then we might at least entertain the notion of Jesus' conversion.

The church's existing Feast of the Conversion of St. Paul the Apostle reminds us that no one turns themselves around under their own initiative. Paul's outlook on life was radically changed by an unexpected encounter with another person—the Lord Jesus. Just so with Jesus' own conversion; it occurred through the agency of the Canaanite woman.

So consider again the Gospel reading for this Feast of the Conversion of Our Lord Jesus Christ.

☙ ❧

Jesus has withdrawn from his homeland of Galilee—maybe to escape the crowds and their demands—and gone off to the foreign region of Tyre and Sidon. A Canaanite woman, a gentile and thus not a member of Jesus' people, comes crying out, shouting even, publicly, in the street, for Jesus to heal her daughter, who is tormented by a demon. Familiar work for Jesus, at least back home among his own people in Galilee. The Canaanite woman keeps crying out—repeatedly—annoying Jesus' disciples until they implore him to send her away, even though she is at home and Jesus is the foreigner. Out there on the street, Jesus does not respond at all to the woman's outcry. To justify his silence, Jesus says to his disciples but not to the woman herself, "I was sent only to the lost sheep of the house of Israel" (Matt 15:24).

Later, inside a house, presumably, the Canaanite woman comes again and, kneeling before Jesus, asks for his help. This time, Jesus does have something to say to her. "It is not fair to take the children's food and throw it to the dogs" (Matt 15:26). An entire ethnic and political outlook on life is packed into this one sentence—an outlook asserting superiority and exclusion. Jesus and his people are the children, the sole and rightful claimants to healing and wholeness. The Canaanite woman and her daughter and all their gentile people are the dogs, unworthy of God's care and advocacy. There is only so much health and worth to go around, and Jesus knows where the line of separation is drawn.

The Conversion of Jesus

Inside the house, the Canaanite woman adopts a different strategy to secure Jesus' help. Having called attention to her need on the street, she now stops shouting. She chooses not to push back directly at Jesus' superior and exclusive words with a demeaning insult of her own. Nor does she allow his words to silence her. Instead, she nonviolently, but irresistibly, deflects Jesus' words and reflects them back to him—transformed. "Yet even the dogs eat the crumbs that fall from their masters' table" (v. 27). Gentle but courageous. A bit of common wisdom she and Jesus can share, despite the line of separation between their peoples, their histories, and their religions. These words of the Canaanite woman turn Jesus around, change his mind and outlook on life radically. "'Woman, great is your faith!'" he replies. "'Let it be done for you as you wish.' And her daughter was healed instantly" (v. 28). That's the conversion of Jesus.

Prior to his conversion, Jesus' words and even his silence are all three times "No!" to the Canaanite woman. *Not* a single word did he answer her. *Not* sent to any except the house of Israel. *Not* right to throw the children's food to the dogs. The Canaanite woman also addresses Jesus three times. Her words are affirmative and invitational. They even anticipate liturgical language we use to this day. *Have mercy on me, Lord. Lord, help me. Eat the crumbs that fall from the table.*[3] The Canaanite woman's words, her faith, her faithful words, convert Jesus. Jesus learns to listen. Jesus learns to see someone from a people other than his own as worthy of health and wholeness, of God's care and advocacy. But only because the Canaanite woman *first* found her voice and used it *both* to cry out *and* to deflect and reflect back words of superiority and exclusion changed into words of inclusion and solidarity.

Matthew sets the stage for this conversion of Jesus earlier in his Gospel when he recalls Jesus drawing the same line of separation between himself and the people of the Canaanite woman. In the story of the sending of the twelve apostles, Jesus gives these instructions, "Go nowhere among the Gentiles, enter no town of the Samaritans, go rather to the lost sheep of the house of Israel" (Matt 10:5–6). Much later, Matthew will attest to the genuine depth of Jesus' conversion. Just before he is arrested and interrogated and executed, Jesus enters the Jerusalem temple—the temple of *his* people—and throws out those buying and selling there—agents of superiority and exclusion among his own tribe, redressing those words about not throwing children's food to the dogs. Having been converted by the great faith of the Canaanite woman, Jesus dares to overturn the tables of the

---

3. Episcopal Church, *Book of Common Prayer*, 356, 117, 337.

money changers, his people again, not foreigners. No longer any talk about crumbs under the table for the inferior and excluded, instead, overturning the very tables of superiority and exclusion themselves. There, toward the end of Matthew's Gospel, Jesus quotes one small portion of our reading this morning from Isaiah to justify his work of throwing out and overturning: "My house shall be called a house of prayer" (Matt 21:13). On this Feast of the Conversion of Our Lord Jesus Christ, we should hear the fullness of Isaiah's words sounding through Jesus' abbreviated quote: a house of prayer "for *all* peoples. Thus says the Lord God, who gathers the outcasts of Israel, I will gather others to them besides those already gathered" (Isa 56:7–8).

※ ※

The collect we prayed at the beginning of this mass asked God for grace "to receive thankfully the fruits of [Christ's] redeeming work, and to follow daily in the blessed steps of his most holy life."[4] Prayed on the occasion of Jesus' conversion, this means receiving the work shared *between* Jesus and the Canaanite woman and following their *side-by-side* footsteps beyond this worship space out into the world. So, I wonder, as individuals and as members of organizations and communities and peoples, where do we need to learn to listen—even, especially, to folk we are tempted to consider inferior and unworthy of care and advocacy? Who among us needs to find their voice? When do our voices need to cry out publicly, and when do words of superiority and exclusion need to be nonviolently, but irresistibly, deflected and reflected back, as an invitation to inclusion and solidarity? And whose great faith might convert us *both* to listening *and* finding a voice, *both* crying out *and* deflecting and reflecting back?

In his *New York Times* op-ed piece this past Tuesday, David Brooks echoes the wisdom shared between the Canaanite woman and Jesus and applies it to the events in Charlottesville, Virginia, and their reverberations throughout the week. Brooks writes:

> The temptation is simply to blast the neo-Nazis, the alt-right, the Trumpkins and the rest for being bigoted, vicious and hated-filled. And some of that is necessary. The boundaries of common decency have to be defined.
>
> But throughout history the wiser minds have understood that anger and moral posturing are not a good antidote to rage and fanaticism. Competing vitriols only build on each other.

---

4. Episcopal Church, *Book of Common Prayer*, 232.

The Conversion of Jesus

In fact, the most powerful answer to fanaticism is modesty.... It means having the courage to understand that the world is too complicated to fit into one political belief system. It means understanding that there are no easy answers ... that can explain the big political questions or existential problems. Progress is not made by crushing some swarm of malevolent foes; it's made by finding the balance between competing truths—between freedom and security, diversity and solidarity....

Modesty means having the courage to rest in anxiety and not try to quickly escape it. Modesty means being tough enough to endure the pain of uncertainty and coming to appreciate that pain. Uncertainty and anxiety throw you off the smug island of certainty and force you into the free waters of creativity and learning.[5]

Modesty, Brooks concludes, is "superior to the spiraling purity movements we see today. It seems like a good time for assertive modesty to take a stand."[6]

ა ა

Now, if we were to keep the Feast of the Conversion of Our Lord Jesus Christ, we might want to have an icon written for the new holy day. I can imagine the Canaanite woman with her assertive modesty front and center. Jesus is there, being turned around to listen to her. The tormented daughter to one side, the annoyed disciples on the other. And in the background, framing the house, a foreign cityscape—quite unlike Jesus' homeland of Galilee or ours here in Seattle: the region of Tyre and Sidon, or, even better for us, maybe, Mogadishu or Kabul.

The idea, the *image*, of writing an *icon* (ha-ha!) for St. Paul's celebration of my proposed new holy day, "The Conversion of Our Lord Jesus Christ," kept enticing me. Eventually, months and months later, I reached out to a wonderfully gifted woman known to me both from St. Paul's and the School of Theology and Ministry: Susan Feiker. Susan is a spiritual director. She is also an artist. Please visit her website: https://www.berkanaspirit.org. In

---

5. Brooks, "Finding a Way."
6. Brooks, "Finding a Way."

So Fill Our Imaginations

fact, she served as artist-in-residence for the entire St. Paul's community—and not just the 5:00 p.m. Sunday mass—during Advent 2016. And so I just up and commissioned Susan to create an icon coming out of my sermon "The Conversion of Jesus" and based on its Gospel text, Matthew 15:21–28. The only other thing Susan had to go on from me were those words at the end of my sermon: "I can imagine the Canaanite woman with her assertive modesty front and center. Jesus is there, being turned around to listen to her. The tormented daughter to one side, the annoyed disciples on the other. And in the background, framing the house, a foreign cityscape—quite unlike Jesus' homeland of Galilee or ours here in Seattle: the region of Tyre and Sidon, or, even better for us, maybe, Mogadishu or Kabul."

Here's a reproduction of Susan's work. Oil and watercolor on an old, burned metal ceiling tile. Measuring twenty-four by thirty-six inches. Amazing, isn't it?

Susan wrote the following reflections in an email to me accompanied by a photo of the icon—my first glimpse of it. The formatting, punctuation, and lack of capitalization are hers.

> a couple of notes about the painting that might be of interest . . . some of these ideas won't come through a black and white photo. but i thought i would tell you anyway just for your knowledge . . . :)
>
> this painting is about 2 feet wide and 3 feet tall. it's painted on an old ceiling tile from a building in pioneer square that had a fire. the black that's in the background is actual soot that i painted on. (there's something about that symbolism that i love)
>
> i asked a friend who 'writes' icons and she told me about some of the symbols of the colors in icons. so even though this isn't a typical icon, i thought i would try and nod to some of the historical ideas that icons displayed. maybe you know some of this . . . but just in case you don't . . .
>
> the outfit of jesus: in icons throughout history he is typically in a red garment with a blue cloak. red signifies humanity and blue signifies divinity (all that is of God, mystery, transcendence). his humanity wrapped in divinity. i realize he doesn't have shoes, but that also lends to the idea of him being more connected to the earth, to the girl (she doesn't have shoes) and to humanity. in his halo, typically there are symbols/letters in the lines. i didn't put those in, but if you would like me to . . . it wouldn't take long for me to add them in. i think it's usually latin or greek letters (probably latin).
>
> the outfit of the lady: i chose green because green signifies life, hope and wisdom. also, in traditional icons, john the baptist is in green symbolizing a truth-teller.

The Conversion of Jesus

The Great Faith of the Canaanite Woman

the girl's outfit: humanity again . . . but also red signifies blood, passion, fire, all this is of the earth. i also researched the term 'canaan' and it might derive from an old term that signifies

So Fill Our Imaginations

the color purple/red because that area was known for using that color of dye. (just an interesting note). with her struggles of demon possession or whatever might have been . . . that is very much struggles of humanity.

also with the girl . . . i wanted to portray her not as a zombie like a lot of images out there portray as demon possession. i was thinking about how maybe she struggled mentally or had some physical ailments that in that time seemed like demon possession. i wanted her to seem frazzled and disoriented . . . with the background behind her and her dress holding a lot of energy making her seem not 'put together' . . . that something was going on with her.

the background (the earth) color: earthly yellow signifies the uncreated light of God's presence. the majority of the painting is in oil, but i painted the background in watercolor . . . with a color that is made out of bronzite, which is a gemstone. its healing energy/properties are for courage and alleviating self-doubt. i see this woman as so courageous to challenge jesus. both as a woman and as a canaanite . . . i think that's pretty amazing of her.

the figures behind jesus (the disciples) and the dog: i wanted to reference the story by having a dog there, but i didn't want to make it prominent. that's why the dog isn't really defined. that's also why i didn't define the disciples. i wanted to have them there but not defined. i wanted to highlight the main characters of the story. kind of like a photo that has the focus of the person or thing you're taking a picture of with the background being kind of blurry. i also wanted to have the disciples with their backs turned walking away.

the symbol at the bottom is the symbol of a couple things . . . one being earth but also one that signifies man and woman coming together. the masculine and feminine. i don't have my book with me right now as i type, but if you want to know more about this symbol, i'll send you the info of what my book on symbols says about this particular one. i think it's called a Wotan cross.

the city: i didn't want to define too much . . . again being kind of like a blurry background to help focus on the main characters. i looked at photos of different muslim cities and found those shapes in the architecture. this particular skyline is, i am sure, nowhere to be found anywhere. i did that purposely to nod to a muslim city but it to not be one that anyone would recognize.[7]

After contemplating the photo of Susan's icon for a few days, I sent her an email, which in addition to all my wonder, thanks, and praise—among other things, for not "drench[ing] Jesus and the woman and the daughter

---

7. Susan Feiker, email to author, June 20, 2018.

in white-ness"—did pose a question that was on my mind: "What I was most hoping for is that you would take the story as an artistic opportunity/challenge to make the most of. I had my little vision of what such a new and edgy icon might include. And you've certainly taken those thoughts about as far as they can go. My big question to you would be, were there other thoughts or impulses you had that are *not* currently reflected in the work; that you didn't incorporate because you were too constrained by my suggestions? If there are, I'd love to hear about them. So, if there's anything else that came to you in the process, I'd love to hear/see."[8]

Her response reassured me and reminded me of what it's like to preach from the lectionary: "in regards to your question of if i was constrained in any way by your suggestions . . . i wasn't. :) if anything, it gave me a good structure to work within being that i was being stretched. but within that structure i found lots of ability to move and be creative. there wasn't anything i wish i could have added in or done differently. i love symbolism, so the things i was thinking about and intrigued by i put in symbolism . . . and i loved that. oh, and i was very intentional on trying to not have jesus, the woman or the girl be 'white'. i'm glad you appreciated that! that's something i have such a hard time with . . . people in the US thinking Jesus was 'white.'"[9]

I did ask Susan to add the traditional Greek letters to Jesus' halo. Ὁ ὬΝ. A kind of caption meaning "the one who is." The Johannine *egō eimi* (I AM). *Adonai* or *HaShem*, that not-to-be-pronounced divine name consisting of those four mysterious consonants, in the Hebrew Testament of Christian Scripture. Which for me deepens, even as it more firmly grounds, the wondrous scandal that Christ Jesus, the very one who is, was converted by a woman, a Canaanite woman. Susan and I agreed, upon further reflection, that the work, the icon—especially because of its impending life beyond my original sermon—should be called "The Great Faith of the Canaanite Woman." And with Susan's permission, and that of Mother Sara Fischer our rector, the icon was placed in both St. Paul's worship spaces (upstairs and downstairs) on Sunday, September 9, 2018, when, now in Lectionary Year B, we heard the Gospel of Mark's version of the story. Her image—Susan's and the Canaanite woman's—has so filled my imagination that it now stands in emblematically for the entire year of preaching.

As you read above, this sermon was originally composed, delivered, and received a week after the oh-so-public white supremacist demonstrations in

---

8. Author's email to Susan Feiker, June 25, 2018.
9. Susan Feiker, email to author, June 30, 2018.

So Fill Our Imaginations

Charlottesville, Virginia, and attendant violence. Donald Trump's response immediately thereafter marked for me one more in a series of early, clear indications of what his presidency would mean for the country. The *Access Hollywood* tape. The inauguration and inaugural address and bickering about the size of the crowd compared to Barack Obama's. The firing of FBI Director James Comey. And Charlottesville: there were "very fine people on both sides."[10]

While sitting with the Canaanite woman and her daughter during my composition process, I was moved by Heather Heyer's mother's words of *both* defiance *and* compassion after her daughter's death in Charlottesville. Heather's mother was quoted as saying:

> This is just the beginning of Heather's legacy. This is not the end of Heather's legacy. You need to find in your heart that small spark of accountability. What is there that I can do to make the world a better place? What injustice do I see?
>
> And you might want to turn away—"I don't really want to get involved with that. I don't want to speak up. They'll be annoyed with me. My boss might think less of me."—I don't care. You poke that finger at yourself, like Heather would have done, and make it happen. You take that extra step. You find a way to make a difference in the world . . .
>
> So remember in your heart: If you're not outraged, you're not paying attention. And I want you to pay attention, find what's wrong, don't ignore it, don't look the other way. You make a point to look at it and say to yourself, "What can I do to make a difference?," and that's how you're going to make my child's death worthwhile.
>
> I'd rather have my child, but, by golly, if I have to give her up, we're gonna make it count.[11]

I wonder why it never occurred to me, however, to research what womanist scholarship has to say about this Canaanite woman, given the context of race and white supremacy in America?[12]

---

10. Thrush and Haberman, "Giving White Nationalists."

11. Durkee, "Heather Heyer's Mom," paras. 10–11, 16–17.

12. For example, as I learned much later, St. Clair, *Call and Consequences*. Now, while this is a commentary on the Gospel of Mark, St. Clair's words might have provided insight into a womanist rereading of Jesus and Matthew's Canaanite woman.

10

Refusing to Play the Payback Game [Remarks for Shared Homily]
The Fifteenth Sunday after Pentecost

Here's another sermon launched by a movie. *War Games*.[1] I had carried an image from that film in my mind for years: a map of the world covered over by lines representing nuclear missile strikes, offensive and retaliatory. And the movie's punchline about global thermonuclear war: "A strange game. The only winning move is not to play." Image and line just waiting for this Sunday's Scripture readings and the theme of forgiveness.

I confessed to you that Matthew had *never* been my favorite Gospel. I wonder if you begin to see the fruits of my repentance in some of these sermons? I must acknowledge, however, that Matthew 18 *has* always intrigued me. And that a few years before the twelve months of preaching explored here, I did some exegetical work with that chapter in connection with a series of adult formation sessions at St. Paul's entitled "Blessed Are the Peacemakers: Matthew's Vision of an Ethical Life." Let's plan on returning to that work in my conclusion to the entire year of preaching.

---

1. Badham, dir., *War Games*.

So Fill Our Imaginations

"Refusing to Play the Payback Game"
[Remarks for Shared Homily]
The Fifteenth Sunday after Pentecost; Proper 19A
Genesis 50:15–21; Psalm 103:8–13; Romans 14:1–12; Matthew 18:21–35
September 17, 2017

Do any of you remember the movie *War Games*? I know, if you're under thirty years of age, you weren't even born when the movie was released—back during the Cold War between the United States and the Soviet Union. *War Games* tells the story of a high school computer nerd from Seattle and his girlfriend who hack into a top-secret military system and find themselves playing a game called "Global Thermonuclear War." The problem is that the supercomputer has also been programed to replace human operation of the U.S. nuclear weapons arsenal and is poised to launch a real war. The two teenagers end up at an underground command center in Colorado to try to prevent this.

Each time the computer explores a scenario, a war game, a Soviet first strike, say, or one by a NATO ally of the U.S., a bright line traces an arc across a huge map of the world representing a nuclear missile that lands and destroys its target. Immediately, two lines arc back in the opposite direction as the other side retaliates. Then four, then dozens, hundreds, back and forth, until the globe is covered by a mushrooming canopy of simulated missile strikes. The computer learns with fantastic speed and runs through possible scenarios faster and faster: an incident in Iran, one in Korea, a missile launch from a submarine, an airplane—always followed by those same lines engulfing the map, and a message on the screen, "Winner: None." No matter where or how the nuclear war begins, the result remains the same: mutual destruction of the United States, the Soviet Union, and their allies. As the countdown to real war accelerates, our high school heroes trick the computer into recognizing the futility of a different game, tic-tac-toe, played intelligently, with its inevitable stalemate. Having completed its long list of war game scenarios—so fast that each iteration of those lines arcing across the globe flashes like a strobe light—the computer concludes: "A strange game. The only winning move is not to play. How about a nice game of chess?" The only winning move is not to play. With that, the system shuts down, and the world is saved.

Refusing to Play the Payback Game

Each of our Scripture readings this evening addresses a game I want to call "Payback." In this game, too, the only winning move is not to play. For to forgive means to refuse to play the Payback game.

In our reading from Genesis, Joseph's brothers fear that he will pay them back in full for the wrong they did by selling him into slavery (Gen 50:15–21). The brothers beg for and receive Joseph's forgiveness. You intended to do me harm, Joseph says, but God coaxed good out of your evil, as I became second-in-command over all Egypt and was here with resources to offer you food and refuge when you and your clan fled Israel during a time of famine.

Psalm 103 should put to rest any fear that God plays Payback with human beings: "God has not dealt with us according to our sins, nor rewarded us according to our wickedness" (Ps 103:10). Instead, "as far as the east is from the west, so far has God removed our sins from us" (v. 11).

For Paul, in Romans 14, the Payback game amounts to one group holding in contempt those who believe or behave differently. Some members of the Christian community at Rome feel themselves free to eat all foods without scruple; others abstain from certain foods as a matter of religious principle. "Let all be convinced in their own minds," Paul allows (Rom 14:5). Paul's concern is that "those who eat must not despise those who abstain; and those who abstain must not pass judgment on those who eat; for God has welcomed them" (v. 3), welcomed *both* groups. Those who eat, every bit as much as those who abstain, do so in honor of Christ Jesus, giving thanks to God.

Peter just itches to play Payback in our Gospel reading: "Lord, if another member of the church sins against me, how often should I forgive? As many as seven times?" (Matt 18:21) "Not seven times, I tell you," Jesus replies, "but seventy-seven times" (v. 22). Peter's question is a setup. Lord, we have a conflict here; I am in the right—totally. Someone else in the church has wronged me: how long must I wait before paying the other back in kind? Will seven times do, and then I can finally give him what he deserves? No, sorry, Jesus says; the Payback game has no place among my own. Seventy-seven times! Which is to say, neither you nor your opponent will ever find a winning move in this game—sooner or later, you will both suffer the spiritual and relational and communal equivalent of mutual destruction. To forgive means *not* to play Payback at all.

And to make sure Peter gets the point, Jesus tells that parable of a king who wants to settle accounts, reckon up all that is owed to him, and have

So Fill Our Imaginations

the debts paid in full (Matt 18:23–35). A first debtor owes an astronomical sum. Of course, he can't pay it back—and, threatened with being sold into slavery together with wife and children, he begs for mercy. The king releases him and forgives the debt. But this forgiven debtor has learned nothing about the Payback game, for, as he leaves the palace, he meets someone who owes him a paltry sum. The first debtor treats the second exactly as he begged not to be treated by the king. He insists upon payment and has the other thrown into prison. What are the limits of forgiveness, you ask, Peter? What is absolutely the longest time you must defer payback to one who has wronged you? Jesus answers: in the kingdom of God, forgiveness knows no statutes of limitation!

In trying to disable the Payback game, this evening's Scriptures confront situations of inequality between people and issue the call to forgive in order to protect the weaker, more vulnerable person or group from the predations of the strong. None of these readings, for example, would ask a battered woman to stay with her abuser, instead of safeguarding her life and health. It is Peter, Jesus' second-in-command, who must forgive—not the less influential member of the church who has wronged him. A great king forgives the massive debt of a helpless slave, who then pays back an even more vulnerable debtor owing a tiny debt. "Welcome those who are weak in faith," Paul writes, "but not for the purpose of quarreling over opinions" (Rom 14:1). Joseph, more powerful than anyone else in Egypt except the Pharaoh himself, forgives his brothers—foreigners, refugees, dependent for their very survival. Instead of clenched fists or fingers poised on launch buttons, we are invited to hold our hands open, cupped upward, able to hold the vulnerable other, gently, gratefully, and then to let go and let be, confident that God's love holds all that we love and all that we lose.

So I wonder, when have you seen the lines of the Payback game arcing across your relationships, your communities, your world? I wonder what forgiveness looks like for you as an alternative to Payback? And I wonder who has mentored you in forgiving? I invite your responses.

As a maturing preacher (hopefully!), I have begun to learn the difficult skill of letting brilliant insights and rich resources go when they don't fit in or just clutter up a particular sermon. In part, that's why I keep a theological,

Refusing to Play the Payback Game

spiritual, and homiletical sketchbook. My sketchbook now has these quotes from Archbishop Desmond Tutu and Dietrich Bonhoeffer on forgiveness left over from "Refusing to Play the Payback Game." Perhaps they will find a place in a subsequent sermon.

Tutu: "Forgiveness is the only way to heal ourselves and to be free from the past. Without forgiveness, we remain tethered to the person who harmed us. We are bound to the chains of bitterness, tied together, trapped. Until we can forgive the person who harmed us, that person will hold the keys to our happiness, that person will be our jailor. When we forgive, we take back control of our own fate and our feelings. We become our own liberator."[2]

Bonhoeffer: "[Jesus] charged us never to tire of forgiving one another. Brotherly [and sisterly and humanly] forgiveness makes room for the forgiveness of Jesus to enter into their common life. Instead of seeing their neighbors as [people] who have injured them, they see them as [people] for whom Christ has won forgiveness on the cross. They meet on the basis of their common sanctification through the cross of Christ."[3]

---

2. Tutu, in Tutu and The Dalai Lama, with Adams, *Book of Joy*, 234–35.
3. Bonhoeffer, *Cost of Discipleship*, 323.

11

Stewarding Our Worth and Inclusion, with Anne Hill Thomson

The Nineteenth Sunday after Pentecost

How is this sermon different from all the others? Well, to start with, I was paired up with a co-preacher. Not just a conversation partner or a member of a lectionary study group during my sermon preparation process, but a second preacher in the pulpit with me that Sunday morning, bringing her own message. Anne Hill Thomson.

For years, St. Paul's has invited lay folk to offer reflections or testimonials during the month of October about what the parish means to them. October—the heart of the stewardship season on the calendar of many Episcopal churches, although the challenge is always to engage stewardship as something more than the annual financial giving campaign. Stewardship, instead, as an ongoing, core aspect of Christian life.

Sometimes, at St. Paul's, these testimonials by lay members of the parish have been freestanding, the homily for the morning or evening; other years, words in addition to the work of one of the regular preachers. Recently, it has been some version of the latter. For example, a sermon by one of the clergy was delivered at its usual time and place in the mass, and then the testimonial giver came up and offered their reflections after communion and before the postcommunion prayer, blessing, hymn, and dismissal. Feedback from the congregation was clear that many experienced those testimonials (wonderful in and of themselves) as disconnected from the liturgy as a whole, especially from the Scripture readings and earlier sermon. So, by

Stewarding Our Worth and Inclusion, with Anne Hill Thomson

October 2017, the stewardship team and the liturgical planners had adopted the practice of working to integrate sermon and testimonial more fully, as part of a single preaching moment, by having the "official" preacher invite the testimonial giver into the pulpit for the final five minutes to conclude the collaborative homily with their words. Mother Sara played this role on two of the three relevant Sundays; me, the other, on Sunday, October 15.

My co-preacher, Anne Hill Thomson, gifted me with the luxury of having a very complete version of her remarks, even though she called it a draft, a week and a half in advance. And her reflections, as you will see shortly, were less a brief testimonial than a full and complete and compelling sermon. It occurred to me immediately that I needed to stay out of the way of Anne's excellent work and just try to provide a frame for it with a few words of mine before and then after her reflections.

I believe this occasion was also the first time I ever preached at both morning and evening services on the same day. Mother Sara and Father Rob have pulled such quadruple duty more frequently. At 7:30, 9:00, and 11:15 a.m. that Sunday, both Anne and I were in the chancel, taking turns seated behind that ship-prow pulpit of ours. After the proclamation of the Gospel, I stepped up into the pulpit and gave my orienting remarks, then invited Anne to take my place while I sat down; she preached her portion of the homily, returned to her seat, and I closed with brief wondering questions. At the 5:00 p.m. mass, which Anne was not able to attend because of her responsibilities as mother of three little boys, I facilitated the shared homily with my opening remarks and closing questions, wrapped around an abbreviated version of Anne's reflections, which I delivered with her permission.

A frame around Anne Hill Thomson's words seemed needed not because of any deficiency in them—rather, because of the challenges posed by Matthew's version of the parable of the wedding banquet that ends up being a parable about the lack of a wedding robe—the Gospel reading for the day. By the time you get to October and stewardship season, by the time you approach the end of Lectionary Year A, congregations and their preachers come face to face with the hardest of the hard sayings of Matthew's Jesus. Sayings involving doors shut. People thrown into outer darkness. Divisions. Separations. Weeping and gnashing of teeth. Lots of deadly violence.

A vineyard owner pays laborers who worked all day in the scorching heat the same wage as those working a single hour (Proper 20). Sheep and goats; those at the right hand of the king and those at the left (Proper 29). The tenants of an absentee landlord who refuse to hand over the produce at harvest time, but beat and kill not only the landlord's slaves but also his son; in response, the landlord "put[s] those wretches"—the tenants—"to a miserable death" and leases the vineyard out to others (Proper 22). The parable of three slaves entrusted with their master's money: five talents, two, and one, as the master goes off on a journey (Proper 28). Five wise and five foolish bridesmaids (Proper 27).[1] Daniel Tidwell-Davis facilitated the 5:00 p.m. shared homily on this last parable and posted his remarks to Facebook, prompting discussion of the apocalyptic Jesus at the end of Matthew's Gospel. I loved the way Daniel flipped our usual expectations, by encouraging us *not* to read Jesus as the bridegroom in the parable—"legalistic, cut throat, and only reward[ing] greed"—but instead as one who announces "a different way of living inside [our] present culture." Announces a God "standing outside the gate with the foolish virgins, and sitting in outer darkness with the servant who was afraid of punishment from the harsh master." Where have we been "wise" in compliance or complicity with what is oppressive in our culture, Daniel asked; and how are we "being invited to become foolish in order to join with God in a different kind of kin-dom?"[2]

But Daniel's remarks still lay four weeks out from Sunday, October 15, and Proper 23 and the parable of the wedding banquet/wedding robe. Because Anne Hill Thomson's reflections on her experience at St. Paul's led her to the reading from Isaiah 25 and not to Matthew 22, and with the words of Jesus' parable still echoing in the worship space(s) when I stepped up (or sat down) to preach, I felt it important to acknowledge the difficulty and suggest a possible way to reconnect the end of the parable to the language of grace otherwise flowing through the mass and its Scripture readings. For I had also been mulling over a beginning-of-the-academic-year devotional my wife, Dr. Debra-L. Sequeira, had given a few weeks earlier at her

---

1. These numbered propers provide a convenient and consistent way to keep track of the Scripture readings appointed for the season after Pentecost in the Episcopal version of the common lectionary. Because the date of the day of Pentecost varies from church year to church year—because the date of Easter Sunday is variable—the number of Sundays making up the season after Pentecost can swing from twenty-three to twenty-eight. See how that could get confusing real quick? Other versions of the common lectionary, Roman Catholic and Presbyterian, for example, employ a slightly different ordering/numbering schema to accomplish the same end. Instructions about this are sprinkled through the Book of Common Prayer; see 15–16, 31–32, 158, 227–36, 879–85, 888, 896–900. For an excellent treatment of how the common lectionary works, as well as basic differences between Roman Catholic and Anglican/Protestant versions, see West, *Scripture and Memory*.

2. Daniel Tidwell-Davis, Facebook post on Nov. 12, 2017.

university, in which she spoke about both high expectations, the high expectations Jesus sets for his followers, and Jesus' insistence that the nature of God is pure gift for all, especially for the last and the least; that having high expectations for ourselves does not mean faster, bigger, biggest. Her thoughts called to mind Paul Tillich's sermon "You Are Accepted."[3] And Dietrich Bonhoeffer's claim that while *free*, the grace of God is never *cheap* but *costly*.[4] All this material, however, remained behind in my study (on my kitchen table, actually) and did not figure in my preaching.

I will have an afterword concerning the reception of this sermon/shared homily, afterwards. After you have read "Stewarding Our Worth and Inclusion."

"Stewarding Our Worth and Inclusion,"
with Anne Hill Thomson
The Nineteenth Sunday after Pentecost; Proper 23A
Isaiah 25:1–9; Psalm 23; Philippians 4:1–9; Matthew 22:1–14
October 15, 2017

[Mark Taylor]

Just to acknowledge up front that you have co-preachers this morning—me and Anne Hill Thomson. Actually, she'll be shouldering most of the load. I'll try to clear a space for her words.

Throughout October, many voices and many hands around St. Paul's help us explore the theme "stewardship for a time such as this." Today's readings and prayers seem to be mostly about grace. I wonder how these themes might weave together? Stewardship and God's gift of life and love, worth and inclusion?

In our collect, we prayed that God's grace might "always precede and follow us."[5] In our reading from Isaiah and in our psalm, grace is imaged as a feast of rich food and well-aged wine for all peoples, a table spread in the presence of all that troubles us (Isa 25:6, Ps 23:5). And we have Jesus'

---

3. In Tillich, *Shaking of the Foundations*, 153–63.
4. Bonhoeffer, *Cost of Discipleship*, 45–48.
5. Episcopal Church, *Book of Common Prayer*, 234–35.

So Fill Our Imaginations

parable of a royal wedding banquet in our reading from Matthew's Gospel (Matt 22:1–10). All the invited guests—family, government officials, leading citizens—refuse to come and celebrate. So, the king reaches out to the streets and, surprisingly, generously, includes all those both good and bad, strangers, the powerless, the poor, as worthy of celebrating, and the wedding hall is filled. Grace, right; amazing grace?

Except that's not where the parable ends. The king notices a man among the guests not wearing a wedding robe: "'Friend, how did you get in here without a wedding robe?' And he was speechless" (Matt 22:11–13). We may be left speechless, too, when the man is bound hand and foot and thrown out. A parable of unexpected inclusion undercut by shocking exclusion?

Much work might be done to contextualize the hard ending of this parable within Matthew's storytelling and Jesus' first-century Middle Eastern culture. Instead, I just want to offer one suggestion. What if, what if the man, beyond all expectations invited to the royal wedding banquet, simply could not or would not steward his own worthiness, his being included? Could not, would not steward the gift of life and love by showing up with his party clothes on, ready to join the other guests in celebrating, to eat and drink and dance? The man entered the wedding hall, but what if he excluded himself from the banquet by *not showing up as a wedding guest*?

Anne Thomson has words around what it might mean to show up stewarding our God-given worth and inclusion. Anne.

ও ও

[Anne Thomson]

In 1979, my parents walked through the doors of St. Paul's with a one-and-a-half-year-old daughter in tow. My name is Anne Thomson (although many of you still think of me as Anne Hill), and I am now here with my own one-and-a-half-year-old.

In 2006, I was invited to give a homily like this. A year earlier, I had moved back to Seattle after spending nine years on the East Coast. I had an apartment on Queen Anne, I was settling into a new job in a new field, and I was establishing a group of friends. I was eager to meet new people, and I had recently started a twenties/thirties group at St. Paul's.

As I reflect on the last eleven years, much has changed in my life: I've had a wedding and three baptisms in this building. I now live on Mercer

Stewarding Our Worth and Inclusion, with Anne Hill Thomson

Island with my husband James and our sons Felix (age five), Toby (age four), and Jasper, one-and-a-half. I am a stay-at-home mom. On the teeter-totter of time, I seem to have flipped from being the child toddling across the threshold of the church to the mother trying to keep my own kids from wiggling in the pew.

The most special and memorable thing about growing up in this parish was the feeling of belonging and being respected, even as a child. It felt special to have adults who weren't related to me acknowledge me, see me, and listen to me—to feel like I was a full member of this community with a voice that was heard. When I was an acolyte, Linda and Kim would show me where to stand and what to do. When I was the crucifer, Herman would show me how to carry the cross at just the right height so it wouldn't hit the choir loft. When I wrote the Christmas pageant, Charlie and Josie typed it up and directed it. Deacon Mary Drew showed me how to read a lesson. And when I went off to Wellesley College, Father Moore's wife Mary mailed me a sugar bowl she had stolen from the dining hall fifty years earlier when she had been a student there. I think of these people and many others often as I look back on being a child here; I remember being a little person looking up to these adults. Most of these people that I just mentioned did not have children of their own, and yet they took an active interest in raising the children of the parish. Some of these people have died, some have moved to other parishes, all would probably be surprised to hear their names mentioned this morning, but I do so to honor them and to remind us that we each have the opportunity to make a mark in the lives of the children of this parish, regardless of whether we are parents. It delights me that my sons are now finding their own place in this community—they look forward to seeing Missy at Godly Play on Sundays, and they have taken pride in baking communion bread with John Sutherland, insisting that I ask him for the recipe. B. J., who taught me Sunday school lessons, now teaches them. They are making friends and forging relationships as their own people.

The second thing that was formative about going to St. Paul's as a child was getting out of the homogeneous community of Mercer Island where I grew up. As a child, to see the city in the early morning hours of Easter Sunday or at midnight on Christmas Eve, was eye-opening. To experience the dichotomy of leaving a family gathering where I had just opened Christmas presents and had a hot meal surrounded by a loving family, and then twenty minutes later, be walking past a man sleeping on the sidewalk made me fully aware of my good fortune and at the same time start to feel a real sense

So Fill Our Imaginations

of social responsibility. To learn about HIV and AIDS in a suburban school is abstract, but then to attend funeral services of friends and parishioners who had died of the disease was real. To have those hard conversations with my parents reminded me of my privilege. And now, how do I explain to my boys why some people don't have homes or enough to eat? How do we as Christians live the lessons we hear on Sundays and, as a parish, how do we raise the children of St. Paul's to be aware and empathetic human beings?

Sometimes, I think of St. Paul's as a relay race where the baton is passed from person to person. There were times when I could participate more, when I could volunteer more, when I could just do *more*. Now, it feels like a win just to get three boys dressed and to church on time. After almost six years of motherhood and sleep deprivation, it feels like an effort just to stand here and string coherent sentences together. As I read the announcements and see all the wonderful things happening in this parish, I am grateful for all of the people who are able to give time to make our parish a community—gardeners who keep our labyrinth neat, bakers who provide communion bread, those who cook for the homeless or wash vestments or serve on our vestry or teach Godly Play—the list goes on. The baton passes from person to person when they have the time and energy to give their gifts. Regardless of whether I can give my time, I pledge my money, so that all of these things can keep happening. And when I write my check, I write it with gratitude for all the people who are able to do more and with apologies that I can't do more at this time.

In the reading from Isaiah we heard:

> For you have been a refuge to the poor,
> a refuge to the needy in their distress,
> a shelter from the rainstorm and a shade from the heat.
> When the blast of the ruthless was like a winter rainstorm,
> the noise of aliens like heat in a dry place,
> you subdued the heat with the shade of clouds;
> the song of the ruthless was stilled. (25:4–5)

With so much ugliness in our world right now, I find myself turning inward, wanting to keep my own family safe and protected. Most days, I feel paralyzed, even though I know, now more than ever, we need to speak up for what is right. As I search for my voice, I am grateful for all the voices of St. Paul's who are always fighting against injustice and who carry the baton when I cannot. I am grateful for St. Paul's continued commitment to helping our homeless neighbors, to advocating for environmental issues, to marriage equality, and for the parish's commitment to all progressive social justice issues. On Sundays, I am grateful to be in this safe and calming place, to sit in silence and stillness with each of you, to express gratitude for the good in my life, to pray for peace and justice in our broken world; and for an hour and a half on a Sunday morning, the song of the ruthless is stilled, as we sit in community with one another.

ഗ ര

[Mark Taylor]

So I wonder, how do you, how do I, show up included and worthy to celebrate at the wedding banquet that is St. Paul's and our lives? Worthy and included with more time and energy or with less? Worthy and included to pass the baton to others or to pick it up and run with it? Either way, worthy and included—because God's grace always precedes and follows us.

There was an edge in the room after I delivered an abbreviated version of the foregoing as my remarks for the 5:00 p.m. shared homily. Several people who spoke during the communal response period expressed profound discomfort with the parable and its exclusion of the guest without a wedding robe. Even angry rejection of such exclusion. There was noticeably more conflict and divergence than usual between and among the eight or ten responses to my words and Anne Hill Thomson's. At first, this made me uncomfortable, even though I've long since learned to trust the process of our shared homily and accept whatever is said as part of the community's authentic engagement with Scripture and occasion. The more I thought about it, however, the more appropriate the responses, especially the angular ones, seemed. *If* the parables of Jesus are not benign or banal little moralistic illustrations, but are meant to be "destabilizing," as Sallie McFague argues; and *if* they work according to "a pattern of orientation, disorientation, and reorientation: the parable begins in the ordinary world with its conventional standards and expectations, but in the course of the story a radically different perspective is introduced, often by means of surrealistic extravagance, that disorients the listener, and finally, through the interaction of the two viewpoints tension is created that results in a reorientation,

So Fill Our Imaginations

a redescription of life in the world."[6] We should be made uncomfortable, if not angry, by a deconstructive boomerang like the parable of the wedding robe/wedding banquet coming around to strike us in the back of our heads.

But still, what about grace? What enables me (you? us?) to hang in there long enough with the hard parables of Jesus not just to become *disoriented* but *reoriented* as well?

The offertory hymn at the 9:00 and 11:15 masses the morning of October 15—after Anne Hill Thomson and I had preached our collaborative sermon and just before we gathered for our eucharistic banquet—was #321 in the Episcopal Church's *Hymnal 1982*. The tune is "Rockingham," with the words of the first three stanzas by Philip Doddridge (both music and text of late eighteenth to early nineteenth-century provenance):

> My God, thy table now is spread, thy cup with love doth overflow;
> be all thy children thither led, and let them thy sweet mercies know.
>
> O let thy table honored be, and furnished well with joyful guests;
> and may each soul salvation see, that here its sacred pledges tastes.
>
> Drawn by thy quickening grace, O Lord, in countless numbers let them come
> and gather from their Father's board the Bread that lives beyond the tomb.

Grace, the last word?

---

6. McFague, *Models of God*, 50; but see the entirety of ch. 2, from which this discussion of the parables comes.

12

Mending What Fear Has Buried
[Remarks for Shared Homily]
The Twenty-Fourth Sunday after Pentecost

I wish I were more regular at journaling. Oh, for years now, I have had a lined composition book set aside for that purpose. But if you look at the far-flung dates of the meager number of entries therein, it appears it takes something fairly extraordinary to motivate me to reflect and record. My journal actually looks more like a sketchbook. And I don't always carry it with me, because it is stuffed with notes written on other pieces of paper—envelopes, worship bulletins, agendas, handouts, cards—whatever was in front of me when I had a thought I wanted to write down and preserve.

Sketchbook? Something I've mentioned several times now. What's that about? My brother-in-law Nick Blosser is a painter. He goes nowhere without his sketchbook—just a tiny little spiral-bound pad of blank paper. In which he'll sketch in pencil a single object: a leaf, a hydrangea blossom, an azalea bush; or a whole beach scene with mountains in the background. Nick sketches these images quickly, just trying to capture their gist. Later, on larger paper, in some cases, he transforms pencil sketch to watercolor drawing. Then, still later, maybe, into a full-sized egg tempera painting on a wooden board—which is his go-to medium. My theological, spiritual, and homiletical sketchbook intermittently tries to do the same with words, sentences, ideas, insights, and visual images, capturing them for future use in class sessions, sermons, academic writing, etc. Many never find a life beyond the sketchbook.

So Fill Our Imaginations

I made the following sketch for November 19, 2017, and the 5:00 p.m. mass at St. Paul's when I was to facilitate the shared homily (Twenty-Fourth Sunday after Pentecost):

- what were Jesus' first followers so afraid of that they might have been tempted to bury the gift? / [that they were] Galileans in Jerusalem
- what might Matthew's community have been so afraid of that they were tempted to bury the gift? / a marginal community facing oppression (just keep quiet—low profile)
- all of these final parables in Matthew [are] about custodians of other peoples' stuff = not *their* treasure, but theirs to maintain, even flourish / all [these parables] oppose a *failure* to make something with what does not finally belong to *them*
- Scripture as gift (?) / how do we steward it?

Clearly, in the lead-up to composing my homiletical remarks, it was the line from Jesus' parable of the talents (Matt 25:14–30) about the third slave being "afraid" of his master that most intrigued me. And I was still wrestling with our reception of the hard sayings at the end of Matthew's Gospel and the end of the church year. Amazingly, almost effortlessly on my part, things fell into place over two days through my interaction with gifts from three other people or groups.

On Tuesday before this next to the last Sunday on the church calendar, my sermon preparation process came around full circle, or maybe spiraled back on a different level. In mid-2017, after six years, I had stepped out of the role of director of worship at school, and the lectionary study gatherings at noon went on hiatus. But, around the same time, Mother Sara began convening a similar homiletical group at St. Paul's. Our practice came to be a brief review of the sermons preached the previous Sunday (morning and evening), followed by a look at what the congregation might need to hear from the readings for the upcoming Sunday. Ideally, all the preachers for both Sundays would be present, almost always including the rector and/or (new) associate rector. A few other folk like me had standing invitations to attend. Well, looking toward Sunday, November 19, we talked a lot about *fear*.

In addition to his timely, challenging blogposts, my successor as director of worship—the Rt. Rev. Dr. Edward Donalson III, theologian, liturgist, writer, and black Pentecostal bishop—initiated bi-weekly, first-thing-in-the-morning coffee and prayer gatherings in the main hallway of our building on campus: Agape Latté. That Tuesday morning, November 14, Edward built his prayer around bell hooks on *fear* and love. I incorporated some of hooks's words into my remarks for Sunday's shared homily.

Then a third and final gift. The next day, on Wednesday, one of my DMin students, Michelle Mope Andersson, presented and defended her project orally. Her research involved stories from the Korean diaspora. Michelle had lived for several years in Pyongyang, the capital of North Korea—one of a very few Americans so situated. I had read Michelle's descriptions of the Japanese artform *kintsugi*—mending broken porcelain pots and cups with gold—in earlier drafts of her project. And she had mentioned an exhibition of the work of Korean artist Yeesook Yung that adopts and adapts *kintsugi*. But until I saw the PowerPoint slides in Michelle's presentation and heard the ultimate use to which she put Yee's huge, mended kimchi pots in interpreting the lives and spiritualities of Korean emigrants to the United States, I hadn't understood their power and brilliance. I hope my remarks in "Mending What Fear Has Buried" pay appropriate tribute.[1]

"Mending What Fear Has Buried"
[Remarks for Shared Homily]
The Twenty-Fourth Sunday after Pentecost; Proper 28A
Zephaniah 1:7, 12–18, Psalm 90, 1 Thessalonians 5:1–11, Matthew 25:14–30
November 19, 2017

Late in each church year, we have a Sunday that directs us to the theme of Scripture. We pray in our collect to the "blessed Lord, who caused all Scripture to be written for our learning."[2] But, year in and year out, this Scripture-focused Sunday offers up some of our most difficult and challenging readings from Scripture. And so, this Sunday evening, what might it mean to "hear, read, mark, learn, and inwardly digest" that reading from Zephaniah, or Psalm 90, or the parable of the talents from Matthew—above

---

1. Mope Andersson, "Treasure in Earthen Vessels."
2. Episcopal Church, *Book of Common Prayer*, 236.

So Fill Our Imaginations

all, to learn and digest these Scriptures as *hope*-full? I have three thoughts to share, and then I look forward to your reflections.

ಬ ಲ

"Cultures of domination rely on the cultivation of fear as a way to ensure obedience." So writes bell hooks, African American author and intellectual, in her book *All about Love*. Cultures of domination cultivate fear. hooks goes on: "In our society we make much of love and say little about fear. Yet we are all terribly afraid most of the time. As a culture we are obsessed with the notion of safety. Yet we do not question why we live in states of extreme anxiety and dread. Fear is the primary force upholding structures of domination. It promotes the desire for separation, the desire not to be known. When we are taught that safety lies always with sameness, then difference, of any kind, will appear as a threat. When we choose to love we choose to move against fear—against alienation and separation. The choice to love is a choice to connect—to find ourselves in the other."[3]

ಬ ಲ

"I was afraid," the third slave in this evening's parable explains to his master, "and I went and hid your talent in the ground. Here you have what is yours" (Matt 25:25). Despite its irresistible meaning in modern English, Jesus and Matthew would have known a talent as a measurement of weight—about seventy-five of our pounds—and then secondarily as a unit of monetary value equal to that weight in silver or gold, hundreds or even thousands of coins. In our parable, the talents belong to the master, not the three slaves, although the talents are entrusted to the slaves, each according to their ability. Each slave has the capacity and the full right to put their master's treasure to work. The first two slaves immediately connect with other people and share, invest the five talents and the two talents, doubling their master's money, and then are invited themselves into the master's joy. Slaves no longer? Friends instead?

The fearful third slave digs a hole in the ground and buries the one talent—the hundreds or thousands of gold or silver coins with which he was entrusted. He feared his master for driving a hard bargain. Perhaps he feared failing. He did the safe thing: he buried the talent. He kept himself separate from other people. He refused to allow himself and his gift to be

---

3. hooks, *Love*, 93.

Mending What Fear Has Buried

known. But our parable suggests that to secure a gift by burying it is to lose the treasure. (Not unlike the plan before Congress to tax university endowments—the gifts of benefactors already given—while eliminating the deduction for future charitable giving.) To share a valuable gift, to invest it in and with others, is to gain even more value. (Like the five loaves and two fish Jesus takes, blesses, and breaks.) In burying the talent, the third slave buries something of himself, buries pieces of a broken self. Fear paralyzes the third slave and makes of him a hoarder—hoarding what was a gift from another. The first two slaves are energized by the audacity of hope. Audacious sharing rather than fearful safety—maybe that's the hope offered up by our parable of the talents.

∽ ∾

In the traditional Japanese artform called *kintsugi*, broken, imperfect, discarded porcelain vessels are mended with thin ribbons of gold enamel.[4]

Kintsugi

A contemporary Korean artist, Yeesook Yung, takes *kintsugi* to an audacious new level. She doesn't just mend individual broken tea cups or

---

4. See Furrow, "Kintsugi for Code."

So Fill Our Imaginations

teapots, she assembles huge five-, six-, seven-foot-tall pillars made up of hundreds of broken vessels—all restored, all recreated, all connected to each other and held together as one by gold. This matters because of centuries of Japanese domination of the Korean people. Because of an old prejudice against the Koreans as too primitive to craft real porcelain "china," viewing the Koreans as capable of making only earthen vessels. Because Yeesook Yung in her *kintsugi* recreations particularly chooses to mend broken kimchi pots, vessels meant to be buried underground until the cabbage and chili mixture ferments—particularly chooses to mend these traditional Korean earthenware pots with gold.[5]

༄ ༄

So I wonder, when have you, when have we, buried something valuable out of fear, doing the safe thing, only to lose the gift altogether?

And where have you, where have we, experienced the *kintsugi* of God's grace—mending the broken pieces of our fearful, earthenware lives with audacious gold?

I invite your responses: to my thoughts, to our difficult and challenging Scripture readings this evening, or to this occasion—the next to the last Sunday of the old church year.

I wrote earlier about the way Sunday Evenings at St. Paul's occasionally makes use of the work of artists-in-residence. I now want to say with regard to the foregoing twelfth and final sermon in the series, that the context of worship downstairs at 5:00 p.m. encourages my own fuller creativity as a preacher. The shared circle of worshippers around the altar and across from one another, along with the shared homily, conspire to bring out the artist in me.

---

5. See Moon, "Artist Yeesookyung."

Mending What Fear Has Buried

Yeesook Yung's Adaptation of *Kintsugi*

So Fill Our Imaginations

Not just hearing the word, for instance, but allowing us to get physical with it. Once, to facilitate the evening community's engagement of the story of Jesus restoring the sight of Bartimaeus from Mark 10, I intentionally wore my woolen sport coat so I could take it off and toss it to the floor at the words: "And they called the blind man, saying to him, 'Take heart: get up, he is calling you.' So throwing off his cloak, he sprang up and came to Jesus" (vv. 49–50). Another time, as a way into Jesus' parable of the Pharisee and the tax collector who went up to the temple to pray (Luke 18:9–14), I invited the worshippers around me to get up out of their seats—if they so chose—and try on the very different postures adopted by the two men: the Pharisee who stood right up as close as he could to the religious action, head held high; and the tax collector, standing far off, not willing to lift his eyes to heaven but beating his breast. I had a hunch that with half a dozen actors in the room, they'd be willing to play along. They were!

I've made objects central to my preaching by setting them on the altar in our midst during the shared homily. The three-foot-tall wooden crucifix that otherwise hangs by the entry door of the downstairs worship space in a sermon that had something to do with Jesus' death on the cross. Ceremonially lighting a votive candle placed inside a holder made out of a block of pink Hawaiian salt and leaving it on the altar throughout my remarks and the community's response to our Gospel reading about being the salt of the earth and the light of the world (Matt 5:13–16). I invited their reflections with some words about light shining through all the facets and textures and colors, yes, and through the blemishes and cracks and imperfections of this salt of the earth.

And I've printed images out on paper and had them in the hands of participants in the shared homily. A textbook diagram of the life cycle of a wheat plant to accompany John 12:24: "Unless a grain of wheat falls into the earth and dies, it remains just a single grain." To anchor a shared homily on the transfiguration of Jesus (Luke 9:28–36), sparked by the Greek of the key line, "the *eidos* of his *prosōpou . . . heteron* / the look of his persona was altered," a picture of Lady Gaga at the Golden Globes on one side of a piece of paper and the character Ally she plays in the movie *A Star Is Born* on the other. I remarked that in playing the unknown Ally, Lady Gaga (= Stefani Joanne) was playing herself before her own star was born and before adopting the persona of Lady Gaga. And as the character Ally's singing career begins to shine on screen, Ally adopts elements of Lady Gaga the actor's offstage persona. Ally's hairstyle and colors grow more like Lady Gaga's, as do her makeup and wardrobe and even her carriage and attitude. Or, finally, the images you viewed accompanying the preceding remarks of a typical example of *kintsugi* side by side with Yeesook Yung's mended tower of unearthed kimchi pots. I've learned—not unlike teaching Godly Play—that it's much easier for me to remember and deliver my homiletical lines without a written script when I have images or objects or bodily postures/gestures to prompt and carry me.

The upstairs worship space on Sunday mornings, with pews and communion rail and platform and pulpit, is less conducive to such nonverbal creativity during a sermon. Or, I am not adept enough at leveraging that space. The closest I've been able to come is to have a photograph of a desperate man being gently talked back and saved from jumping off the Golden Gate Bridge by a first responder reproduced on a two-foot-by-three-foot foam core board and displayed on an easel in the upstairs entryway (not in the worship space itself), or a drawing of mine for what I dubbed "In Between Sunday" (the Sunday after the ascension of Jesus but before the descent of the Spirit on Pentecost) available as a printed handout after mass, again in the entryway, and just mentioned in passing during the sermon. I wonder if this has something to do with why my Sunday morning preaching has often exercised *subsequent* agency, addressing unfinished creative business, and led to the writing, after the fact, for example, of the icon of the great faith of the Canaanite woman? And I wonder how, in order to mitigate feeling like a homiletical figurehead on the prow of a ship, I might bring still more of myself as downstairs Godly Play teacher, facilitator-of-shared-homily, and artist-in-residence up with me into the pulpit on Sunday mornings?[6]

---

6. Surprisingly enough, my experience of preaching at St. Paul's virtual Sunday worship services during COVID-19 restrictions has begun to close the gap between what used to be my morning sermons and my remarks for shared homily in the evenings and to open up new imaginative opportunities.

Conclusion

The Work and Play of Preaching

I OFFERED YOU THE foregoing twelve sermons because they belong together. Because they trace one preacher's year—one parish community's year, one city's, one country's. A church year. A year of life in the world.

Now that you have read my sermons, I wonder what you see and hear and feel? What strikes you? What draws you in? What bumps you out?

I wonder about relationships between my preaching and my theologizing. I do *not* see much technical, academic theological jargon in these twelve sermons. Instead, I *do* see my underlying, operative theology being carried by certain knots of images. The pregnant, whispering possibilities of darkness; its productive uncertainty; the capacity of nighttime to protect even as it hides us; signs, dreams, angels. Daylight; noonday brightness; exclusive certitude and conformity that blind; or/and, insight, new discovery, discovery of the new, the true, birth and rebirth. Theology carried by prepositions, even. Jesus present *between* us as community. *Beyond* the fences of hatred and control. God *in* whom we live.

I'm struck by the gerunds, those verbs shapeshifting as nouns, in my sermon titles. *Seeing. Walking. Touching. Stewarding. Mending.* Frequently, I seem to try and embed church-y words and concepts otherwise. *Compassion*—of course, but *visceral* compassion? *Face-to-face* and *hands-on* compassion that is nevertheless *limitlessly expansive*? Not just Paul's conversion, but *the conversion of our Lord Jesus Christ* himself? Forgiveness as *refusing*

Conclusion

to play the Payback game? The broken parts, the fragments, of ourselves and our communities fear *buries*?

I notice the biblical characters who appear in these sermons. Those with names: Jesus and Peter and Paul. Ahaz and Joseph and Mary. Nicodemus and Thomas. And those left unnamed. Someone who sowed good seeds in their field. A guest not wearing a wedding robe. Slaves entrusted with talents, five and two and one. More telling, the young woman who is with child, and the Canaanite woman and her daughter. I'm drawn in by lines from Scripture that lend titles to entire homiletical occasions. The unknown God "in whom we live and move and have our being." "Let both of them grow together until the harvest."

The lasting impression I carry away from the composition and delivery, reception and subsequent agency of these twelve sermons, however, has to do with the juxtaposition of work and play, play and work.

I relish the irony that in a program of religious formation named Godly *Play*, the children's response to the word, the story, is called their *work*. Just in my brief experience as a Godly Play instructor in one parish, this work can take the form of drawing, embroidery, modeling items out of clay, building balsa wood structures, painting, creating dozens of tiny little thyme leaves with a fine-tipped green marker and "grinding" them with a mortar and pestle to make a poultice for the blind girl in the story of St. Valentine (my closed eyelids stood in for the girl's), or just marching the figurines of the people of God through the sand of the desert box (okay, to be honest, often burying them). The artistic response, the imaginative, open-ended activity following the *play* of hearing a lesson presented is dubbed the children's *work*. Thereby, for me, both work and play are taken out of their normal (adult) contexts and radically transgressed, reversed, redefined. Deconstructed and reconstructed. Work and play, play and work: another binary *queered*! Playful work. Working play.

Playful Work

At my best, my most imaginative and open-ended, the earnest adult work of composing these twelve sermons has been child's play. Multiple forms of play. Yes, of course, the sermons did not just materialize out of thin air. I worked to get to them in response to contexts and texts. For several, this involved something akin to *collage-making*. Finding and then taking found objects, found images, cutting them out, trimming them and arranging

So Fill Our Imaginations

them together. The blog post, "God in Disguise." Antonio Machado's poem on how walking makes the way. A *New York Times* op-ed by David Brooks after Charlottesville. Once, I invited elements for the collage through Facebook (patron saints, St. Paul as patron). And, three times, I was given items by others that needed to be incorporated into and with what I had to say. The work of the artists-in-residence: Anne Doe-Overstreet's poem concerning Nicodemus and Christine Brown's scene from the life of Dorothy Day. Anne Hill Thomson's homily that required only appropriate framing, offering the congregation a way in and a way forward.

Each Sunday, the appointed Scripture readings from the lectionary represented givens this preacher had to work with. Givens defined by the Episcopal Church and its prayer book and shaped by communal expectations at St. Paul's. I wrote earlier that a crucial aspect of my sermon preparation process is the hour or so of free play with one or more of the lectionary texts. Wondering about them or wandering with them. Often some lexical work with key Greek words behind a passage in the English Bible. Or literary play with imagery and structure. Playful work with where a particular story from John's Gospel, say, sits within the arc of the placement and progression of all the other stories. With truly beneficial or blessedly useless examination of the Synoptic Gospels to track down if a text in Matthew, for instance, has a parallel in Mark and/or Luke. If not, wow—a uniquely Matthean feature! If so, how similar and different are the accounts in the two (three) Gospels? In either case, clues about Matthew's distinctive take on Jesus, his words and work, his significance for our lives and times. Or just an outline of narrative elements or a cloud of half a dozen strong images, named, circled, and laid out on paper, so I could visualize their interrelationships.

To illustrate, here are copies of two pages of notes? sketches? mockups? that came out of the hour or so of wondering and wandering with the story of the Canaanite woman and Jesus.

Handwritten. Always handwritten. I am never at my best, most imaginative or open-ended while sitting at a keyboard. Mechanical pencil, 0.7 mm, and fine-point pens in various colors (green, purple, teal). Jesus off in the territory of Tyre and Sidon in Matthew 15, with a glance back at his command in Matthew 10 to his disciples to go nowhere among the gentiles and ahead to Matthew 21, with Jesus quoting Isaiah to the effect that God's house shall be called a house of prayer. Except that Matthew omits the phrase "for all the nations [peoples]" found in Mark and retained from

Conclusion

Isaiah. But then Matthew in chapter 27 *does* tell the story of the gentile centurion at Jesus' crucifixion and, in chapter 28, passes along Jesus' commission to his followers to go and make disciples of *all* nations.

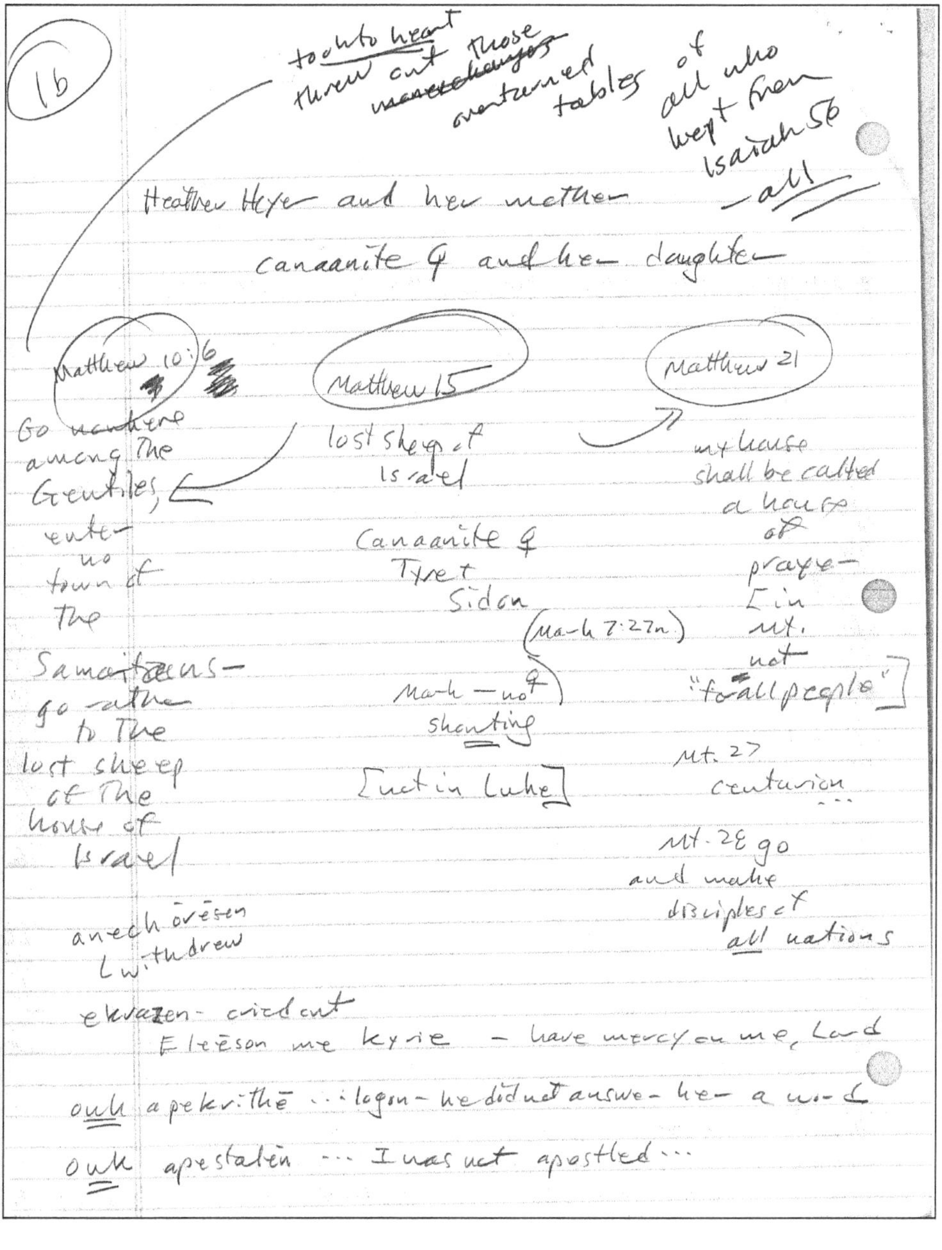

[Handwritten notebook page, numbered 16, with notes on Matthew 15 and related passages:]

- took to heart / threw out those / overturned tables / all who wept from / Isaiah 56 — *all*
- Heather Heyer and her mother
- Canaanite ♀ and her daughter

Matthew 10:6
Go nowhere among the Gentiles, enter no town of the Samaritans — go rather to the lost sheep of the house of Israel

anechoresen / withdrew

ekrazen — cried out
Eleēson me kyrie — have mercy on me, Lord
ouk apekrithē ... logon — he did not answer her a word
ouk apestalēn ... I was not apostled ...

Matthew 15
lost sheep of Israel
Canaanite ♀
Tyre + Sidon
(Mark 7:27n)
Mark — no ♀
shouting
[not in Luke]

Matthew 21
my house shall be called a house of prayer
"in mt. not 'for all people'"

Mt. 27 centurion

Mt. 28 go and make disciples of *all* nations

Wondering and Wandering with Matthew 15

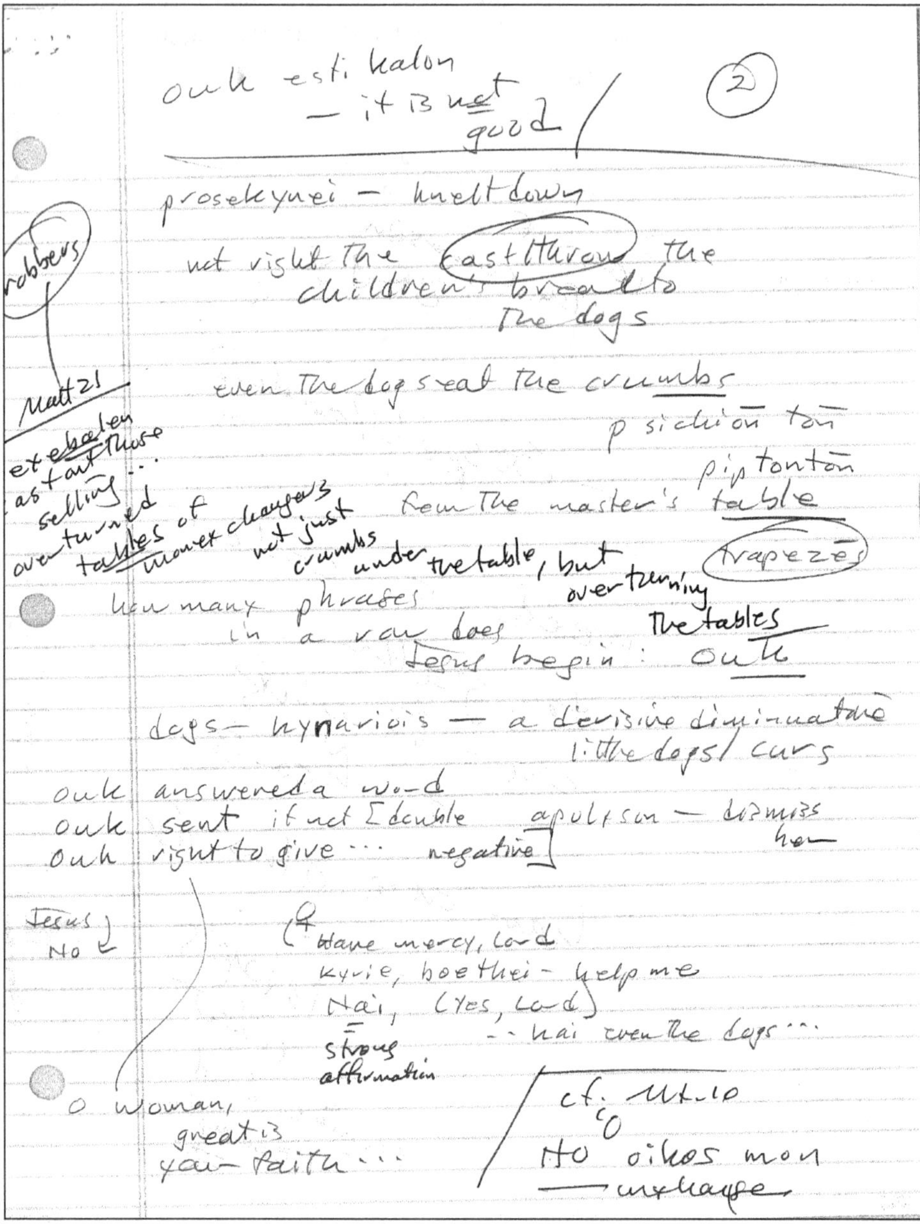

So Fill Our Imaginations

(handwritten notes, page 2)

ouk esti kalon
— it is **not** good

prosekynei — knelt down

not right the **cast/throw** the
children's bread to
the dogs

even the dogs eat the crumbs

psichion tōn
piptontōn
from the master's table
not just
crumbs under the table, but
overturning
how many phrases the tables
in a row does
~~Jesus~~ begin : ouk

robbers

Matt 21
exebalen
as tas those
selling
overturned
tables of
money changers   trapezes

dogs — kynariois — a derisive diminutive
                                    little dogs / curs

ouk answered a word
ouk sent   if not I double   apolyson — dismiss
ouk right to give … negative]   her

Jesus)
No (
       (Have mercy, Lord
        kyrie, boethei — help me
        Nai, (Yes, Lord)
        =
        strong
        affirmation   -- nai even the dogs …

O woman,   cf. Mt 10
   great is   "O
   your faith …   Ho oikos mou
                        — my house

More Wondering and Wandering

Conclusion

And my Greek word play. *Anechōrēsen* (withdrew). *Ekrazen* (cried out). *Kynaria* (dogs, little dogs, curs). That important verb: to cast or throw (*balein*); eating the crumbs (*psichiōn*) that fall from their master's table (*trapezēs*)—anticipating Matthew 21 and Jesus' casting out (*exebalen*) those who sold and bought in the temple and overturning the tables of the moneychangers, echoing Jesus' work of casting out (*ekballei*) demons in Matthew 8, 9, 12, and 17. But especially the careful structure in Matthew 15 of Jesus' threefold response to the Canaanite woman's plea, each beginning with *ouk* (not). *Ouk apekrithē autē logon* (not answered he a word); *Ouk apestalēn* . . . (not apostled [sent] was I to any but the house of Israel); and *Ouk estin kalon* . . . (not is good/right to cast/throw the children's bread to the dogs). Matched by the woman's triple, and triply assertive, reply: *Eleēson me, Kyrie*; *Kyrie boēthei moi*; and *Nai* (strong affirmative *yes*!), *Kyrie, kai gar ta kynaria esthiei apo tōn psichiōn tōn piptontōn apo tēs trapezēs tōn kyriōn autōn*. Which reminded me of lines from the prayer book: "Lord have mercy."[1] "O Lord, make haste to help us."[2] "We are not worthy so much as to gather up the crumbs under thy Table."[3]

Now I occasionally make collages in real life. My playful work with scriptural texts feels different from collage-making. What artform might it resemble, instead? Let's see. Done by hand. Using a fine-pointed instrument. Lots and lots of material to start with—much more than remains in the finished product. A creative process of paring down, whittling away, honing in, until a recognizable shape emerges from the unruly mass. Wood *carving*, maybe?

Some exegetical carving I did years earlier with Matthew 18 for that series of adult formation classes at St. Paul's stands behind the tenth of these sermons, the one for the Fifteenth Sunday after Pentecost in the evening. I have alluded several times to treating Mark 5 in my school of theology and ministry classes as a chapter emblematic of major themes across the entire Gospel (the stories of the demon-possessed man living among the tombs, the woman with the hemorrhages, and the synagogue leader Jairus and his dying daughter). John 9, with its story of Jesus healing the man born blind, might play a similar role within the fourth Gospel. Until I played around with it seriously, I had no idea Matthew 18 could also be considered such a

---

1. Episcopal Church, *Book of Common Prayer*, 356.
2. Episcopal Church, *Book of Common Prayer*, 117.
3. Episcopal Church, *Book of Common Prayer*, 337.

So Fill Our Imaginations

chapter. Both encapsulating Matthew's story of Jesus and projecting ahead to the community around Matthew decades later.

At first glance, Matthew 18 looks a lot like the lost-and-found box outside the Godly Play rooms downstairs at St. Paul's—filled with a jumble of mismatched items. I count at least seven distinct elements making up this thirty-five-verse chapter:

1. The question of who is greatest in the kingdom of heaven, which Jesus answers by posing a child to his (adult) disciples (vv. 1–5).
2. Beware of putting stumbling blocks in front of such little ones—better to have a millstone strapped on and be thrown into the sea (vv. 6–7).
3. If your hand/foot causes you to stumble, cut it off and throw it away; if your eye, tear it out (vv. 8–9).
4. The shepherd leaving ninety-nine sheep to search for the one stray (vv. 10–14).
5. What to do if another member of the church sins against you: go to them privately; then, if need be, bring one or two witnesses along; finally, go public with the communal breach. Which has something to do with binding and loosing in heaven as on earth, as well as with where two or three are gathered in Jesus' name (vv. 15–20; is this one single element or three?—which, if three, would bring the total for Matthew 18 to nine).
6. (or is it eight?) Peter's question about how many times he must forgive another member of the church (vv. 21–22).
7. And, finally, seven (or nine?). Jesus' parable of the king and the slave whose massive debt of ten thousand talents was forgiven, only to turn around and demand full repayment from a fellow slave of a measly one hundred denarii (vv. 23–35).

Many of these elements are unique to Matthew. Others shared with Mark and/or Luke are placed in proximity to each other uniquely in Matthew. To borrow the language of bird-watching: these are diagnostic field marks of Matthew's theology and spirituality, the distinctive features that allow sure identification of a bird as belonging to this species, not some other.

In his telling, Matthew consistently leads with Jesus as teacher. We might discern five primary collections of rabbi Jesus' sayings that structure and propel Matthew's narrative. Chapters 5–7, of course, our Sermon

Conclusion

on the Mount—a mountain, note, in Galilee. Chapters 10, 13, and 18 (our focus here). And chapters 23–25, the increasingly conflictual sayings of Jesus, after he has arrived in Jerusalem—including many of the hardest of his hard parables. I notice the way Matthew calls attention to the shifting audience(s) of Jesus' teaching and arranges the material in quasi-chiastic fashion reflective of an outside-inside, public-private dialectic:

- Chapters 5–7: sayings to Galilean crowds and Jesus' own disciples
- Chapter 10: to Jesus' twelve disciples
- Chapter 13: parables before great Galilean crowds, backed up by private instruction for the disciples
- Chapter 18: to disciples and Peter
- Chapters 23–25: sayings to Judean crowds (and their leaders, the scribes and Pharisees) and the disciples

So, Matthew 18 with its seeming lost-and-found box of elements is addressed simultaneously to Jesus' innermost circle of disciples and the church of Matthew's day. Which helps expose at last Jesus' central message throughout the chapter, expressed in that odd and oddly chilling tenth verse: "Take care that you do not despise one of these little ones; for I tell you, in heaven their angels continually see the face of my Father in heaven." The little ones face to face with God. Children. The one lost sheep over against the ninety-nine. The slave owing a hundred denarii and refused forgiveness by the other slave, the one just liberated from his ten-thousand-talent debt. And which also suggests that Jesus' words about stumbling blocks and millstones, about cutting off hands and feet and plucking out eyes, about Peter—possessor of the keys to the kingdom—needing to forgive a member of the church who sinned against him seventy-seven times, not seven, *are all meant to protect the most vulnerable within the community against the predations of the stronger, the privileged.* Providing testimony, once again, of the formative influence of the resources of feminist and womanist theologies upon my playful work—here, in relation to how I read Scripture.

But to be clear about my original point, note how much carving it took to arrive at this honed conclusion from Matthew 18 for the sake of remarks facilitating the shared homily on the evening of the Fifteenth Sunday after Pentecost, September 17, 2017.

So Fill Our Imaginations

Working Play

On three occasions, my work, my response to the biblical text(s) within our contemporary context(s), continued to play out way beyond the composition and delivery, even the initial reception, of a particular sermon or shared homily. These three preaching moments exercised notable subsequent agency.

I did finally get to create that image suggested by the movie *The Founder* of the golden arches of McDonald's between the cross and the Stars and Stripes (recall the sixth sermon in the series, "To an Unknown God in Whom We Live and Move and Have Our Being"). The opportunity arose when I had to build a website on the Canvas learning platform for the introductory preaching class I was to teach at school. I couldn't quite literally sandwich the golden arches between the cross of Christ and the American flag, but I came close.

Between the Cross and the Stars and Stripes

Conclusion

What do you see in the result? An infographic for dominant American cultural values? A social/political/economic critique? An invitation to engage preaching with politics, politics with preaching? Indirect, in any case, for better or worse.

In two cases, I enlisted others in even more substantial and creative working play. I have already written amply about Susan Feiker's icon of the great faith of the Canaanite woman that emerged from "The Conversion of Jesus," sermon number 9. Let's now consider the subsequent agency of the eighth in the series, "Let Both of Them Grow Together until the Harvest."

I began my remarks for the 5:00 p.m. shared homily on the Seventh Sunday after Pentecost (July 23, 2017) holding one of the golden parable lesson boxes from Godly Play on my lap. While I made it clear that the parable of the weeds among the wheat—the Gospel reading for that Sunday—is not one of the parables offered to children in the Godly Play curriculum, I did want to frame our adult engagement of the parable with some of the actions and words from Godly Play around how hard it can be, sometimes, to find our way into the parables of Jesus. (For your information, the six core Godly Play parable lessons present Jesus' parables of the good shepherd [itself a collage of Matt 18:12–14, Luke 15:1–7, Psalm 23, and John 10], the good Samaritan, the great pearl, the sower, the leaven, and the mustard seed. There are also five enrichment lessons, including one on the rabbinic parable of the deep well.)[4] Later, I thought it would be fun and challenging and fruitful to create a full Godly Play lesson on the parable of the weeds among the wheat. I wanted to try to imagine how children might respond to it, so I could better find my own way in.

I knew I would need help on this project. I turned to one of several gifted Godly Play instructors I know, Melissa (Missy) Trull. Missy had been involved in children's religious formation at St. Paul's for years, most recently as lay pastor for the program. Missy was also a student at Seattle University's School of Theology and Ministry where I teach, completing the course work for her MDiv chaplaincy degree in spring 2018. She graciously accepted my invitation to play along. So, we got to work.

All we had for a starting point were these few stage directions from my remarks for that shared homily: "If this had been a real Godly Play parable lesson," I wrote, "inside the box there might have been a brown cloth underlay for the field, figures of a sower and an enemy with seeds, wheat plants and weeds all grown up together, and a bundle of weeds and a barn full of

---

4. Berryman, *Complete Guide*, 3:77–131.

wheat." These words and a desire to create as faithful and by-the-book a Godly Play lesson as possible. Missy and I traded first and second drafts of a lesson, writing and rewriting individually, and then sat down together one afternoon to finalize the results of our working play. Here's what we came up with. The format is intentionally very similar to a chapter from volume 3 of the Godly Play curriculum. I do need to acknowledge that Missy Trull and I departed from the NRSV translation of Matthew 13:27 in rendering *douloi* as "laborers," rather than "slaves," and *oikodespotou* as "landowner," instead of "householder," because the parable is about land, the field, not the house/home, the *oikos*. This was for the children's sake, I'm tempted to say. But maybe it was really for our own sake, mine and Missy's, as adults.

Parable of the Weeds among the Wheat
Lesson Notes

Focus: The Weeds among the Wheat (Matt 13:24–30)

- Parable
- Enrichment Presentation

The Material

- Location: Parable Shelves
- Pieces: Parable Box with half-gold and half-green dot; two bags of "seeds" (wheat in bag with gold string, weeds in bag with green string); small oval box with yellowish green sprouts; larger rectangular box with full-grown wheat plants (gold) and weeds (green)
- Underlay: brown

Background

The three Synoptic Gospels, along with the Gospel of Thomas, present an overlapping—yet enticingly nonidentical—collection of parables of Jesus. Matthew gathers them all together in one place in the narrative (ch. 13), as does Mark (ch. 4). Luke divides them between two chapters (8 and 13).

Conclusion

Versions of these same parables can be found scattered throughout Thomas, which consists entirely of sayings of Jesus, without narrative structure or context.

In the canonical Gospels, the parable of the weeds among the wheat is unique to Matthew (13:24–30). It does appear in Thomas (saying 57). This parable immediately follows Matthew's version of the parable of the sower (and allegorical explanation, from Jesus? the early church?). Matthew separates the parable of the weeds among the wheat, however, from its explanation by the intervention of several other parables.

Here's how the Synoptic Gospels and the Gospel of Thomas arrange their nonidentical but overlapping collection of parables:

> Matthew 13—parable of the sower / why parables? / explanation of sower / parable of the weeds among the wheat / parable of the mustard seed / parable of the yeast / why parables? / explanation of weeds among wheat / parable of the treasure hidden in a field / parable of the great pearl / parable of the net / why parables?
>
> Mark 4—sower / why parables? / explanation of sower / parable of the lamp / parable of the seed growing secretly / mustard seed / why parables?
>
> Luke 8—sower / why parables? / explanation of sower / lamp; Luke 13—mustard seed / yeast
>
> Thomas—net (saying 8) / sower (9) / mustard seed (20) / lamp (33) / weeds among wheat (57) / great pearl (76) / yeast (96) / treasure in field (109)

Most interesting, perhaps, is the parallel position (and role?) of the parable of the weeds among the wheat in Matthew and the parable of the seed growing secretly in Mark—both following the parable of the sower (and explanation) and furthering it? pushing back against it?

The enemy in the parable sows the seeds of a plant that looks like wheat but is not wheat at all. It is called darnel (*Lolium temulentum*), and it is a weed. People should not eat darnel. It can be poisonous, especially if infected with an endophytic fungus of the genus *Neotyphodium*, as is often the case. A Roman law forbade the sowing of darnel in a neighbor's wheat field. These historical matters may not be interesting to children, but they are mentioned to invite the reader to discover more about this parable as an adult.[5]

---

5. See "*Lolium temulentum*" and Krantz, "Parable."

So Fill Our Imaginations

Notes on the Material

Find the material in a gold parable box with a half-gold and half-green dot, located on the second shelf of one of the parable shelves. The underlay is brown felt in an irregular shape. There are two small canvas bags, differentiated only by the color of the string that holds each bag closed: one gold, the other green. The bag with the gold string holds the good "seeds" (wheat); the one with the green string holds the "seeds" of the weeds. There is also a small oval box holding the sprouts of wheat and weeds (both identically shaped and yellowish-green) and a larger rectangular box holding full-grown wheat plants (gold) and weeds (green).

MOVEMENTS	WORDS
Go to the parable shelves and pick up the parable box. Point to the half-gold, half-green dot on the box that identifies it as the parable of the weeds among the wheat. Bring the parable to the circle of children and place it in the middle.	Watch carefully where I go, so you will always know where to find this lesson.
Lean back and reflect for a moment about what might be inside. Begin when you and the children are ready.	Now, let's see. The box is the color gold. Something valuable must be inside. Parables are very valuable, even more important than gold, so maybe there is a parable inside. It looks old. Parables are old. They are older than you, and they are older than me. They are even older than your grandmother or grandfather. Perhaps there is an old parable inside.
Raise the box and extend it, as if offering it to the circle of children.	The box looks kind of like a present. Parables are like presents. They were given to you even before you were born. They are yours. You don't need to take them. They are already yours, even if you don't know what they are.

Conclusion

MOVEMENTS	WORDS
Press the fingers of one hand against the lid of the box, trying to get inside. Then turn the box around, this way and that, still focusing on the lid.	Look at this lid. Sometimes parables have a lid on them, like a door that is shut. The lid keeps you from going inside the parable. I don't know why. This sometimes happens even if we are really ready, so don't be discouraged. Keep coming back, and, one day, the parable will open up for you.
Take off the lid and leave it tipped against the side of the parable box, next to the children sitting in the circle. This will help the children keep focused on what is being presented rather than what is to come out of the box, and it helps keep the box mysterious.	I have an idea. Let's see what's inside the box. Maybe there is a parable inside.
Remove the underlay. Hold it up and examine it, then drop it in a crumpled shape in the middle of the circle. Smooth it out as you speak. As you wonder, the children may offer their own ideas of what the underlay could be. If there is silence, let there be silence for a while. It is important for the children to know that silence is important and no cause for anxiety.	I wonder what this could be? Maybe it's a chocolate bar. Or, when it is crumpled like this, it could be a rock. I wonder what else it could be? Yes, it could be the dog's blanket. A towel on the floor ready to go in the washing machine. It is brown, the color of dirt, mud, rich soil. It is the color of a field waiting for plants to grow. I wonder what this could really be?

So Fill Our Imaginations

MOVEMENTS	WORDS
	Let's see if there is anything else in here that can help us get ready. Oh no, there isn't anything else! All we can do is begin.
Look back in the box. The pieces left all have to do with the telling of the parable.	There was once someone who said such wonderful things and did such amazing things that people followed him. As they followed him, they heard him talking about a kingdom, but it was not like the kingdom they lived in. It was not like any kingdom anyone had ever visited. It was not even like any kingdom that anyone had ever heard of. They couldn't help it. They had to ask him. What is the kingdom of God like?
	One time when they asked him this, he said, "The kingdom of God may be compared to someone..."
Take the small canvas bag tied with the gold string from the parable box. Untie the bag, scoop "seeds" from it, and motion as if you are spreading them across the field.	"... who sowed good seed in their field."
Take the second canvas bag, the one with the green string, untie it, and again scoop "seeds" from the bag and scatter them in the field.	"But while everybody was asleep, an enemy came and sowed weeds among the wheat, and then went away."
Take the small oval box full of sprouts from the parable box. Place the sprouts throughout the field. All the sprouts are the same color: yellowish-green. Take your time and make sure the sprouts are close together.	"So when the plants came up..."
Take the larger rectangular box of full-grown plants out of the parable box. The wheat plants will be gold, the weeds green. First, place the wheat plants in the field, covering some of the sprouts. The wheat will appear to be growing.	"... and bore grain..."

Conclusion

MOVEMENTS	WORDS
Now, place the weed plants in the field, covering more of the sprouts. The weeds will appear to be growing.	"... then the weeds appeared as well."
Pause for a moment, keeping your eyes on the plants.	"And the laborers came to the landowner and said, 'Did you not sow good seed in your field? Where, then, did these weeds come from?'" "The landowner answered, 'An enemy has done this.'" "The laborers said, 'Then do you want us to go and gather them?'"
Act out what the landowner is saying: Make a "rake" with the fingers of one of your hands and motion to uproot weeds. As you do, pull up wheat plants as well.	"'No,' the landowner replied, 'for in gathering the weeds you would uproot the wheat along with them.'"
Then put both kinds of plants back in place in the field and say:	"'Let both of them grow together until the harvest; and at harvest time, I will tell the reapers: Collect the weeds first and bind them in bundles to be burned, but gather the wheat into my barn.'"

So Fill Our Imaginations

MOVEMENTS	WORDS
	Now, I wonder . . .
	. . . if the person who sowed the good seed has a name?
	I wonder if you have ever seen wheat growing in a field?
	I wonder if you have seen weeds?
Lean back. Look up at the children, make eye contact, and begin the wondering questions.	I wonder if the landowner was happy to see the weeds growing among the wheat?
	I wonder why an enemy would sow weeds among someone else's wheat?
	I wonder if the laborers were happy to let both the weeds and the wheat grow together?
	I wonder if you have ever come close to a place where weeds and wheat both grow together until the harvest?
	I wonder where this whole place could really be?
Reflect for a moment upon all these wonderings. You then begin to put things away, slowly and carefully, one at a time.	While I am putting everything away, please begin to think about what work you are going to get out. Only you know how you would like to respond to the story.
	Watch now where I go to put this parable away, so you will always know where to find it.

I offer up the lesson Missy and I created as a returning gift to Godly Play, to Jerome Berryman, from St. Paul's and especially the Sunday evening worshipping community, in gratitude for all that their playful work and working play have given us liturgically and homiletically and spiritually. Thank you!

Epilogue

Preaching to (My) White Privilege

"SO FILL OUR IMAGINATIONS," pray a few folk preparing to serve in the liturgy on Sunday mornings at St. Paul's during the seasons of Advent and Lent. Except in Eastertide and on high holy days, the entire assembly, *everyone*, morning and evening, confesses their sins against God and neighbor using words such as "by what we have done, and by what we have left undone" or "we repent of the evil that enslaves us, the evil we have done, and the evil done on our behalf."[1]

At the distance of a few years now, I see much left undone in the twelve sermons from 2016–2017. I see enslaving evil. Evil I have done and evil done on my behalf. For, even in connection with my favorite sermon of the bunch, the one on the conversion of Jesus by way of the great faith of the Canaanite woman, I remarked only the words of defiance and compassion of Heather Heyer's mother after her daughter was killed during the white supremacist demonstrations in Charlottesville, Virginia. Indeed, Heather Heyer's death exhibits a tragic and troubling image of contemporary American life. And her mother's words—whatever they were, compassionate or defiant or otherwise—deserve hearing. But why did I gravitate to that one death, the death of that one *white* woman, and those few words, rather than the killing of thousands of African Americans over centuries at the hands of white supremacy? Rather than the many words of their mothers? In my subsequent preaching, white privilege, *my* white privilege, has

---

1. Episcopal Church, *Book of Common Prayer*, 360; *Enriching Our Worship 1*, 56.

So Fill Our Imaginations

become more and more pivotal. Named. Critiqued. Called to repentance and conversion. Offered painful and plenteous redemption.

White privilege called to repentance and offered redemption in anticipation of the fiftieth anniversary of James Forman's "Black Manifesto" delivered during a 1969 Sunday morning worship service at New York City's Riverside Church demanding reparations for slavery and more.[2]

By brilliant lines from student papers on the God stuff in Alice Walker's *The Color Purple*. Quoting a bit of Shug Avery's theology: "I think it pisses God off if you walk by the color purple in a field somewhere and don't notice it."[3] Calling out the false god that long held the main character in the novel enslaved: "Celie's god is powerful, but in a world where all power belongs to men, and more specifically, white men, her god becomes an oppressive white man. He is near enough to talk to, to write prayers to, but not near enough to care about her plight. Her god is a person, but not *her* person." Making application: "As I reflect on the characters and stories in *The Color Purple* and I think about my own life, I believe that the fact that we are able to make it to the other side is a reflection of God's realness and exemplifies God's power to renew and make whole again . . . . There is a kind of joy that surfaces in mourning, . . . that bubbles up as one looks ahead to a long list of daunting tasks, the kind of joy that blocks one from feeling anxiety or anger in the face of hardship and instead lends strength to its recipient."[4]

Exactly four hundred years since the first enslaved African arrived in Virginia, the Rev. Dr. William Barber II, Stacey Abrams, Barack Obama, and Eric Holder repairing the breach, one *poor person*, one *immigrant*, one *voter*, one *law*, at a time.[5]

Through an attempt to preach my own sermon to white America, to myself, in response to the Rev. Dr. Michael Eric Dyson's *Tears We Cannot Stop: A Sermon to White America*. In response to sermons preached in my homiletics class by two African American women—one for a Good Friday Seven Last Words of Christ service (unpacking the second word, "Today, you will be with me": witness to a *right-now God* for a *right-now church*), the other on the empty tomb and the road to Emmaus (what did Jesus do with his resurrected life?—he *showed himself to the disappointed* and *promoted*

---

2. M. L. Taylor, "In the Meantime."
3. Walker, *Color Purple*, 167.
4. M. L. Taylor, "God's Power among Us."
5. M. L. Taylor, "Repairing the Breach One ____ at a Time."

the marginalized women). In response to the Seattle Art Museum's exhibition "Figuring History," of paintings by African American artists Robert Colescott, Kerry James Marshall, and Mickalene Thomas (Feb. 15–May 13, 2018) and the Seattle Repertory Theatre's staging of Christina Ham's play "Nina Simone: Four Women" (Apr. 26–June 2, 2019), making visible so many gifts and graces of black culture previously unseen by me as a white man. In humble response to the blessing of being trusted to learn from the Rt. Rev. Dr. Edward Donalson III and the good folk of the United Ecumenical College of Bishops. And so, ultimately, in response to the story of Saul's blindness on the road to Damascus, even though his eyes were open (Acts 9); how when Ananias laid hands on Saul, something like scales fell from his eyes and his sight was restored; how Saul got up, was baptized, took some food, and regained his strength—so he could begin to proclaim Jesus, instead of persecuting him. Saul no longer, but the apostle Paul. A sermon to myself as a white American, in response to Rev. Dr. Dyson's sermon: be honest. Gain knowledge. Act on what you've learned.[6]

As my contribution to the 5:00 p.m. community's 2019 Lenten journey of protest, petition, and penitence at St. Paul's. An image of my own (hand) making: Mary of Bethany anointing Jesus' feet with costly perfume and wiping them with her hair (John 12).

---

6. M. L. Taylor, "Sermon to White America?"

So Fill Our Imaginations

Mary of Bethany—Letting Down and Lavishing in Love

A wordless protest sign displayed toward the end of my remarks for our shared homily on the Fifth Sunday in Lent. About which I wondered aloud: What do we wear pulled back, tied up, and covered that needs to be let down and lavished in love / while there's still time / so that fragrance might

Epilogue

fill the house? And: When have we seen love beyond measure / beyond cost protest exclusion, scarcity, and self-aggrandizement?[7]

Finally, my sermon for the Conversion of St. Paul the Apostle (transferred) on January 24, 2021.[8] A sermon composed, delivered, and received nearly a year into the novel coronavirus pandemic. In the wake of a summer of reckoning with the fact that Black Lives Matter (and don't!) in America. Days after the inauguration of Joseph R. Biden as president of the United States and Kamala D. Harris as vice president. On the very same Sunday marking four years since Donald J. Trump's inauguration and on the very same Capitol steps that saw the insurrection of January 6. All while the people of St. Paul's continued to worship remotely via Zoom technology with its bizarre blend of visual, facial, and vocal intimacy and on-the-screen human flattening and disembodiment.

This sermon seems particularly replete with images and imagination. Images from the Scripture readings appointed for the occasion, of course. But also a few lines from Joe Biden's inaugural address and from the amazing poem that the amazing Amanda Gorman, national youth poet laureate, read at the inauguration; closing with words from the song Seattle rock band the Foo Fighters performed at Wednesday evening's inaugural celebration. I imagined one of those bronze statues of a Confederate general climbing down off his pedestal; leaving horse and flag behind—that flag with the stars and bars that had so recently been paraded through the U.S. Capitol—casting aside sword and uniform; walking all the way to Washington, DC, in order to take his place at the back of the crowd with other white allies, following the larger-than-death-or-life monument to Martin Luther King Jr. His truth is marching on! I even imagined out loud on Zoom trying to draw something, or paint it, or make a collage depicting an imaginary family tree that would juxtapose a photo of my great-great-grandfather Bushrod W. Taylor's Confederate States of America gravestone in Joyce, Louisiana (he was no general, just a lowly corporal), and the roadside billboards demanding justice for Breonna Taylor, the African American woman killed in her own apartment by Louisville, Kentucky, police.

---

7. Realigning with earlier norms, these remarks were delivered orally (and visually) at the 5:00 p.m. mass on April 7, 2019, but no written version was posted to the St. Paul's website.

8. M. L. Taylor, "Paul's Conversion; and Mine and Yours?" After posting it to the parish website and living with it a while, I subsequently retitled this sermon "Lay Down Our Arms to Reach Out Our Arms."

So Fill Our Imaginations

I can imagine something of the subsequent agency of this final sermon—although such work, such play, still lies ahead for me in the person I hope I'm becoming. Some things in this book brought full circle; others left to spiral outward and away. I invite *your* responses.

Bibliography

Badham, John, dir. *War Games*. Santa Monica, CA: Metro-Goldwyn-Mayer/United Artists, 1983.
Berryman, Jerome W. *Children and the Theologians: Clearing the Way for Grace*. New York: Morehouse, 2009.
———. *The Complete Guide to Godly Play*. 4 vols. Denver, CO: Morehouse Education Resources, 2006–2011.
Bonhoeffer, Dietrich. *The Cost of Discipleship*. Translated by R. H. Fuller. Rev. ed. New York: Macmillan, 1959.
Brancaccio, David. "The True Origin Story behind McDonald's." Marketplace, Feb. 9, 2017. https://www.marketplace.org/2017/02/09/ray-kroc-mcdonalds-fast-food/.
Brooks, David. "Finding a Way to Roll Back Fanaticism." *New York Times*, August 15, 2017.
Bynum, Caroline Walker. *Holy Feast and Holy Fast: The Religious Significance of Food to Medieval Women*. Berkeley: University of California Press, 1987.
Campbell, Ted A. *Christian Confessions: A Historical Introduction*. Louisville, KY: Westminster/John Knox, 1996.
Catherine of Siena. *The Dialogue*. Translated by Suzanne Noffke. New York: Paulist, 1980.
Cone, James H. "Looking Back, Going Forward." In *Shaping a Theological Mind: Theological Context and Methodology*, edited by Darren C. Marks, 1–13. Aldershot, UK: Ashgate, 2002.
———. *Said I Wasn't Gonna Tell Nobody: The Making of a Black Theologian*. Maryknoll, NY: Orbis, 2018.
Daly, Mary. *Beyond God the Father: Toward a Philosophy of Women's Liberation*. Boston: Beacon, 1973.
———. *Gyn/Ecology: The Metaethics of Radical Feminism*. Boston: Beacon, 1978.
"Donald Trump *Access Hollywood* Tape." Wikipedia, last edited Jan. 20, 2022. https://en.wikipedia.org/wiki/Donald_Trump_Access_Hollywood_tape.
Douglas, Kelly Brown. *The Black Christ*. Maryknoll, NY: Orbis, 1994.

Bibliography

Duncan, Lenny. *Dear Church: A Love Letter from a Black Preacher to the Whitest Denomination in the US.* Minneapolis: Fortress, 2019.

Durkee, Alison. "Heather Heyer's Mom Gives Stirring Funeral Speech: 'This is Just the Beginning of Heather's Legacy.'" MIC, Aug. 16, 2017. https://www.mic.com/articles/183859/heather-heyers-mom-gives-stirring-funeral-speech-this-is-just-the-beginning-of-heathers-legacy.

Dyson, Michael Eric. *Tears We Cannot Stop: A Sermon to White America.* New York: St. Martin's, 2017.

The Episcopal Church. *The Book of Common Prayer and Administration of the Sacraments and Other Rites and Ceremonies of the Church.* New York: Church, 1979.

———. *Enriching Our Worship 1.* New York: Church, 1998.

———. *The Hymnal 1982.* New York: Church, 1982.

Fischer, Sara. "Bring It On." St. Paul Seattle, 2016. http://www.stpaulseattle.org/sermons/bring-it-on.

———. "Living Inside Out and Outside In." St. Paul Seattle, 2016. http://www.stpaulseattle.org/sermons/2484273.

———. "Marvelously Made." St. Paul Seattle, 2017. http://www.stpaulseattle.org/sermons/marvelously-made/.

Franklin, R. W. "[Edward Bouverie] Pusey and Worship in Industrial Society." *Worship* 57 (1983) 386–412.

Furrow, Ash. "Kintsugi for Code." Ashfurrow (blog), Feb. 1, 2016. https://ashfurrow.com/blog/kintsugi-for-code/.

Gilligan, Carol. *In a Different Voice: Psychological Theory and Women's Development.* Cambridge, MA: Harvard University Press, 1982.

Goizueta, Roberto S. *Caminemos con Jesús: Toward a Hispanic/Latino Theology of Accompaniment.* Maryknoll, NY: Orbis, 1995.

Grant, Jacquelyn. *White Women's Christ and Black Women's Jesus: Feminist Christology and Womanist Response.* American Academy of Religion Academy 64. Atlanta: Scholars, 1989.

Griffith-Jones, Robin. *The Four Witnesses: The Rebel, the Rabbi, the Chronicler, and the Mystic.* New York: HarperCollins, 2001.

Hancock, John Lee, dir. *The Founder.* New York: Weinstein Company, 2017.

Hatchett, Marion J. *Commentary on the American Prayer Book.* New York: HarperCollins, 1995.

Hayes, Diana L. *Hagar's Daughters: Womanist Ways of Being in the World.* New York: Paulist, 1995.

Hogan, Lucy Lind. *Graceful Speech: An Invitation to Preaching.* Louisville, KY: Westminster/John Knox, 2006.

Holmes, David L. *A Brief History of the Episcopal Church.* Harrisburg, PA: Trinity International, 1993.

hooks, bell. *All about Love: New Visions.* HarperCollins, 2001.

Johnson, Robert A. *Owning Your Own Shadow.* New York: HarperCollins, 1991.

Jones, Susan. "The Forest in the City." *Faith and Form: The Interfaith Journal on Religion, Art, and Architecture* 46, no. 2 (2013) 15–19.

Julian of Norwich. *Showings.* Translated by Edmund Colledge and James Walsh. New York: Paulist, 1978.

Kempe, Margery. *The Book of Margery Kempe.* Translated by B. A. Windeatt. New York: Penguin, 1985.

Bibliography

Kierkegaard, Søren. *Eighteen Upbuilding Discourses*. Edited and translated by Howard V. Hong and Edna H. Hong. Kierkegaard's Writings 5. Princeton, NJ: Princeton University Press, 1988.

———. *Either/Or: A Fragment of Life, Parts I and II*. Edited and translated by Howard V. Hong and Edna H. Hong. Kierkegaard's Writings 3 and 4. Princeton, NJ: Princeton University Press, 1987.

———. *Without Authority*. Edited and translated by Howard V. Hong and Edna H. Hong. Kierkegaard's Writings 18. Princeton, NJ: Princeton University Press, 1997.

Krantz, Jeff. "The Parable of the Wheat and the Tares." Theological Stew (blog), 2008. http://www.theologicalstew.com/wheat-and-tares.html.

Lathrop, Gordon W. *Holy People: A Liturgical Ecclesiology*. Minneapolis: Fortress, 1999.

———. *Holy Things: A Liturgical Theology*. Minneapolis: Fortress, 1993.

Lisa. "God in Disguise." A Sky Full of Stories (blog), Dec. 16, 2014. https://acitygirlacountryworld.wordpress.com/2014/12/16/god-in-disguise/.

"*Lolium temulentum*." Wikipedia, last edited Oct. 15, 2021. https://en.wikipedia.org/wiki/Lolium_temulentum.

McFague, Sallie. *Life Abundant: Rethinking Theology and Economy for a Planet in Peril*. Minneapolis: Fortress, 2001.

———. *Models of God: Theology for an Ecological Nuclear Age*. Philadelphia: Fortress, 1987.

Machado, Antonio. "*Caminante no hay camino*." Poemas del Alma, 1907. https://www.poemas-del-alma.com/antonio-machado-caminante-no-hay-camino.htm.

Melville, Herman. *Moby-Dick; or, The Whale*. Edited by Harrison Hayford and Hershel Parker. New York: Norton, 1967.

Moon, So-Young. "Artist Yeesookyung Translates Korean Tradition in Her Works: 'Nine Dragons in Wonderland' Shown at Venice Biennale." *Korea JoongAng Daily*, May 18, 2017. http://koreajoongangdaily.joins.com/news/article/article.aspx?aid=3033554.

Mope Andersson, Michelle. "Treasure in Earthen Vessels: Stories from the Korean Diaspora." DMin diss., Seattle University, 2018.

Nolan, Albert. *Jesus before Christianity*. 25th anniv. ed. Maryknoll, NY: Orbis, 2001.

Parker, Ned Allyn. "Preaching to Belong: The Practice of Narrative Preaching as an Indicator of Authenticity in the Postmodern Church." DMin diss., Seattle University, 2016.

Ruether, Rosemary Radford. *Sexism and God-Talk: Toward a Feminist Theology*. Boston: Beacon, 1983.

Russell, Letty M. *Church in the Round: Feminist Interpretation of the Church*. Louisville, KY: Westminster/John Knox, 1993.

Rzepka, Jane, and Ken Sawyer. *Thematic Preaching: An Introduction*. St. Louis: Chalice, 2001.

St. Clair, Raquelle Annette. *Call and Consequences: A Womanist Reading of Mark*. Minneapolis: Fortress, 2008.

St. Paul's Episcopal Church. "Anglo-Catholicism." St. Paul Seattle, n.d. http://www.stpaulseattle.org/theology-practice/anglo-catholicism/.

———. *Art around the Parish*. Self-published booklet, n.d.

———. *Renewing St. Paul's for the Next 50 Years*. Self-published building renovation capital campaign case booklet, 2009.

Taylor, Barbara Brown. *Learning to Walk in the Dark*. New York: HarperCollins, 2015.

Taylor, Mark Lloyd. "Almost Earnestness: Autobiographical Reading, Feminist Re-Reading, and Kierkegaard's *Concluding Unscientific Postscript*." In *Feminist Interpretations of Søren Kierkegaard*, edited by Céline Léon and Sylvia Walsh, 175–202. University Park: Pennsylvania State University Press, 1997.

Bibliography

———. "Blessed Are Who?" St. Paul Seattle, Feb. 17, 2019. http://www.stpaulseattle.org/sermons/blessed-are-who/.

———. "The Boundless Love of God and the Bounds of Critical Reflection: Schubert Ogden's Contribution to a Theology of Liberation." *Journal of the American Academy of Religion* 57 (1989) 103–47.

———. *God Is Love: A Study in the Theology of Karl Rahner*. American Academy of Religion Academy 50. Atlanta: Scholars, 1986.

———. "God's Power among Us." St. Paul Seattle, Dec. 17, 2017. http://www.stpaulseattle.org/sermons/gods-power-among-us/.

———. "The Hermit Emerges Victorious: Contempt for Women in Kierkegaard's Attack upon the (Male) Ecclesiastical Establishment." In *"The Moment" and Late Writings*, edited by Robert L. Perkins, International Kierkegaard Commentary 23, 199–238. Macon, GA: Mercer University Press, 2009.

———. "In the Meantime." St. Paul Seattle, July 29, 2018. http://www.stpaulseattle.org/sermons/in-the-meantime/.

———. "Ishmael's (m)Other: Gender, Jesus, and God in Melville's *Moby-Dick*." *Journal of Religion* 72 (1992) 325–50.

———. "Making Room for Others." St. Paul Seattle, Mar. 18, 2018. http://www.stpaulseattle.org/sermons/making-room-for-others/.

———. "Paul's Conversion; and Mine and Yours?" St. Paul Seattle, Jan. 24, 2021. http://www.stpaulseattle.org/sermons/pauls-conversion-and-mine-and-yours/.

———. "Practice in Authority: The Apostolic Women of Søren Kierkegaard's Writings." In *Anthropology and Authority: Essays on Søren Kierkegaard*, edited by Poul Houe et al., 85–98. Amsterdam: Rodopi, 2000.

———. "Repairing the Breath, One _____ at a Time." St. Paul Seattle, Aug. 25, 2019. http://www.stpaulseattle.org/sermons/repairing-the-breach-one-_____-at-a-time/.

———. "'A Sermon to White America?' Remarks for Shared Homily." St. Paul Seattle, May 5, 2019. http://www.stpaulseattle.org/sermons/a-sermon-to-white-america-remarks-for-shared-homily/.

———. "Watching Over." St. Paul Seattle, Nov. 2, 2019. http://www.stpaulseattle.org/sermons/watching-over/.

———. "A Well-Considered Occasion: Kierkegaard and the Wedding Ceremony Prescribed by the 1830 Danish *Altar Book*." In *Three Discourses on Imagined Occasions*, edited by Robert L. Perkins, International Kierkegaard Commentary 10, 245–88. Macon, GA: Mercer University Press, 2006.

———, and Carmen Renee Berry. *Loving Yourself as Your Neighbor: A Recovery Guide for Christians Escaping Burnout and Codependency*. San Francisco: Harper & Row, 1990.

———, and Alissabeth Newton. "Playing with Pictures of Paradox: Children and Christology in Søren Kierkegaard and *Godly Play*." *Journal of Childhood and Religion* 4 (2013) 1–66.

———. "Praying at the Edges: Theology of an 'Emergent,' Anglo-Catholic Sunday Evening Eucharist." *Worship* 90 (2016) 246–69.

Thrush, Glenn, and Maggie Haberman. "Giving White Nationalists an Unequivocal Boost." *New York Times*, Aug. 16, 2017.

Tillich, Paul. *The Shaking of the Foundations*. New York: Charles Scribner's Sons, 1948.

Tutu, Desmond, and The Dalai Lama, with Douglas Adams. *The Book of Joy: Lasting Happiness in a Changing World*. New York: Penguin-Random House, 2016.

Bibliography

Walker, Alice. *The Color Purple*. New York: Harcourt Brace Jovanovich, 1982.

———. *In Search of Our Mothers' Gardens: Womanist Prose*. New York: Harcourt Brace Jovanovich, 1983.

West, Fritz. *Scripture and Memory: The Ecumenical Hermeneutic of the Three-Year Lectionaries*. Collegeville, MN: Liturgical, 1997.

Williams, Delores S. *Sisters in the Wilderness: The Challenge of Womanist God-Talk*. Maryknoll, NY: Orbis, 1993.

Williams, Rowan. "Between the Cherubim: The Empty Tomb and the Empty Throne." In *On Christian Theology*, 183–96. Oxford, UK: Blackwell, 2000.

www.ingramcontent.com/pod-product-compliance
Lightning Source LLC
Chambersburg PA
CBHW051940160426
43198CB00013B/2227